WANGKA

WANGKA

Austronesian Canoe Origins

BY

EDWIN DORAN, JR.

TEXAS A&M UNIVERSITY PRESS   College Station

Library of Congress Cataloging in Publication Data

Doran, Edwin.
 Wangka: Austronesian canoe origins.

 Bibliography: p.
  1. Canoes and canoeing—Islands of the Pacific.
2. Navigation, Primitive—Islands of the Pacific. I. Title.
GN635.I75D67   623.8′29   80-6108
ISBN 0-89096-107-7 (cloth)   AACR2
ISBN 1-58544-086-8 (pbk.)

Manufactured in the United States of America
FIRST PAPERBACK EDITION

To James Hornell
He knew more about primitive watercraft
than anyone else will ever know.

Contents

~~~~~~

Foreword by Ben R. Finney   11

Preface   13

Acknowledgments for Illustrations   15

1. Introduction   19

2. The Canoes   23

3. Historical Sketch of Canoe Theories   46

4. The Anthropological Evidence for Cultural
    Movements   49

5. Seaworthiness of Austronesian Canoes   54

6. The Distributional Evidence   73

7. Ages and Origins   89

Appendix 1. Sources for Distribution Maps   95

Appendix 2. Watercraft Complexity   101

Bibliography   103

Index   107

Illustrations

Three *paraus* off Jolo, Sulu Archipelago.
.... *frontispiece*

                                 Page

   Locations of principal countries, islands,
     and island groups 18
1   Austronesian language phylum 20
2   Three types of Australian bark boats 22
3   Fijian bamboo raft 24
4   Large dugout near Bongao, Sulu Archipelago
     25
5   Modern double canoe analogue
     Hokule'a 25
6   Sail and deck plans, end views, and
     lines of *Hokule'a* 26
7   Sail and deck plans, end views, and
     lines of *Nalehia* 27
8   Double canoes from the Tuamotus and Mailu,
     New Guinea 28
9   The single-outrigger *wa* of Puluwat
     Atoll 29
10 Sail plan of the *wa Mikael* 30
11 Deck plan and float elevations of the
     wa Mikael 31
12 Midship cross-section and lines of the
     wa Mikael 32
13 Hull lines of *Epifano*, another Puluwat
     canoe.......................... 32
14 Single-outrigger canoe from Tahiti 33
15 The *vinta Nardi* off Bongao, Sulu 33
16 Sail plan of the *vinta Nardi* 33
17 Plan, midships section, and lines of the *vinta*
     Nardi 34

18 Double-outrigger canoes from Sulawesi, Bali,
     and East Java 35
19 Diagrams illustrating angle made good
     off the true wind and distance
     made good 37
20 Techniques of tacking and shunting 38
21 Principal Austronesian sail types 40
22 Differences between lateen (lug) sails
     and spritsails 42
23 Primitive crane spritsail on a *tongiaki*, double
     canoe of Tonga, late
     eighteenth century 43
24 Two-masted sailing canoe of Siassi,
     New Guinea 44
25 Racial distributions 50
26 Old Melanesia and Hoabinhia 50
27 Austronesian linguistic relationships 51
28 Distribution of Lapita pottery sites 53
29 Primary Austronesian dispersals in the Pacific
     53
30 Maximum stability in four canoe configurations
     57
31 Stability curves for double canoe
     Nalehia 58
32 Stability curves for single-outrigger
     canoe *Mikael* 59
33 Stability curves for double-outrigger
     canoe *Nardi* 60
34 Polar sailing diagram for three canoes 64
35 Sail balance in four canoe
     configurations 70
36 Distribution of bark boats 75
37 Distribution of wood or bamboo rafts 75

38 Distribution of bark boats and outrigger canoes in Australia 76
39 Distribution of dugout canoes without outriggers 77
40 Distribution of double canoes 77
41 Distribution of single-outrigger canoes and of shunting technique 78
42 Distribution of double-outrigger canoes 79
43 Distribution of the double spritsail 81
44 Distribution of the Oceanic spritsail 81
45 Distribution of the crane spritsail and primitive crane spritsail 82
46 Distribution of boom lugsails 82

47 Distribution of the common spritsail 84
48 Distribution of the quarter rudder 85
49 Distribution of lateral sponsons 86
50 Watercraft complexity based on twelve Austronesian boat traits 87
51 Distribution of end symmetry and hull asymmetry 88

TABLES

1. Data for Canoes of Three Types 63
2. Comparison of Three Hypothetical Canoes 67
3. Summary of Seaworthiness Rankings 71

Foreword

~~~~~~

LONG before the Portuguese and Spanish inaugurated Europe's Age of Exploration, even before the Vikings ventured across the North Atlantic, on the other side of the globe another seafaring race had already spread over two oceans. From a homeland somewhere among the islands of Southeast Asia, or along its continental shores, one branch moved east into the Pacific to find and settle the many islands strewn over that vast ocean, while, later, another branch crossed the Indian Ocean to colonize the great island of Madagascar. The geographical spread of these Austronesian-speaking peoples far surpassed that of the world's next largest cultural-linguistic grouping, the Indo-Europeans. Just take Polynesia alone, the easternmost province of the Austronesian world. The Polynesian triangle, bounded by New Zealand, Hawaii, and Easter Island, would if cast upon Eurasia stretch from England across Europe and Asia to the Aleutians and then south almost to the tip of India!

The sea was the highway that enabled the Austronesians to travel over so much of the globe, and the canoe was their vehicle. Without their innovation of the seagoing canoe, whole stretches of ocean, and archipelago after archipelago, would have been unknown to mankind until the Chinese, Iberians, or some other seafaring people developed their own long-range vessels and sailing skills. But what is this vessel of the Austronesians that crossed oceans before caravels and junks?

Austronesian sailing craft come in many sizes and shapes. The swift "flying proas" of Micronesia, the great double canoes of Polynesia, and the massive double outriggers of Indonesia and the Philippines are the best-known types. These craft have long fascinated foreigners, particularly seamen who appreciate their fine lines, their ingenious construction, and the way they cut so deftly through the sea. This fascination has given rise to a considerable literature of first-hand descriptions by Captain Cook, Admiral Paris, and other early visitors and of various later syntheses.

Yet, despite all the lavish engravings of canoes under sail, despite all the pages describing how they are constructed and how one type differs from the other, the documentary record has some conspicuous gaps. How fast can the canoes sail? How well do they point into the wind? How seaworthy are they? Until recently the literature gave no unambiguous and precise answers to these and other crucial sailing and performance questions. Thus, a debate such as that over the nature of Polynesian settlement could get bogged down for want of necessary data. While advocates of the view that Polynesians settled their island world through a series of planned voyages could pick and choose from ambiguous references just those quotations which would seem to show that Polynesian canoes were fine, seaworthy vessels capable of undertaking voyages of exploration and colonization in any direction and over practically any distance, Andrew Sharp and other critics could dip into the same literature to find support for their view that the canoes were dull sailers and too unseaworthy to allow planned migrations.

It was just a decade ago that Edwin Doran showed us a way out of this impasse by borrowing the techniques and instrumentation of yacht racers and by going out to Micronesia and the Philippines to measure exactly how the canoes of those regions sail. This was no easy task (as I can attest from my efforts to employ the same methods to measure the performance of reconstructed Polynesian double canoes), although Doran's economical prose and concise graphical presentations might give that impression.

But in this monograph Doran goes far beyond summarizing his technical work. The question at hand is the origin and sequence of development of Austronesian canoe types. Doran pays special tribute to James Hornell, the late Director of Fisheries for Madras who was in his time the foremost authority on primitive watercraft, but respectfully differs from him on canoe origins. Or is Doran really arguing with anthropologist A. C. Haddon, the Cambridge don who collaborated with Hornell in their monumental three-volume work, *Canoes of Oceania*? Although it is an invaluable compilation, *Canoes of Oceania* suffers from the anthropological fashion of the day. It was written some fifty-odd years ago when wave theories dominated anthropological work on Pacific prehistory and it was thought that a detailed comparison of artifacts from island to island would reveal the sequence of migratory waves that had populated the Pacific. (Interestingly, in her 1924 Ph.D. dissertation Margaret Mead warned her colleagues that such an approach would be a fruitless endeavor.) Thus, Haddon and Hornell's work is not so much about canoes as sailing craft as it is about how they were constructed, in the hope that similarities and differences between islands would reveal the pattern of migratory waves. Questions of sailing performance and seaworthiness are, for example, virtually ignored in favor of long descriptions and comparisons of such minutiae as how outrigger canoe floats were attached.

Now that the wave theories have subsided, and now that linguistic and archaeological advances enable us to begin to sketch with some confidence the probable migratory routes of the Austronesians, the study of their canoes can be freed from the service of prehistory. Instead, the findings of prehistory, together with those on canoe performance and seaworthiness, can be used to fabricate a new synthesis on where the first seagoing canoes originated and on the sequence of development and diffusion of subsequent canoe types. This is exactly what Doran has so skillfully done in the pages which follow. This work is a labor both of seamanship and scholarship to be appreciated by all who have wondered how ancient mariners, bereft of the technological advantages enjoyed by later mariners, could have joined together wood and fiber to make the sleek canoes that carried them over two oceans.

BEN R. FINNEY

Preface

As everyone knows, a preface should explain how the author came to write his book and then acknowledge the assistance toward its creation given by others. Some prefaces are short, others long and autobiographical. Because a book is a serious piece of work, almost all tend to be solemn. And almost all, as noted by Walter Prescott Webb in his humorous essay "An Honest Preface," tend to be a bit untruthful. I shall attempt to be brief, truthful, and not overly solemn.

My interest in outrigger canoes dates at least from 1937, when, inspired by Melville and Jack London, I added a float to a kayak, persuaded an understanding mother to stitch a sail from old sheets, taught myself to sail from a book, and promptly learned a lesson. From one side it is easy, but tacking a single-outrigger canoe when the float is to leeward is a difficult maneuver. I have been learning more about such craft ever since.

In the more than forty years that have elapsed, I have sailed many kinds of boats and built half a dozen double outriggers (trimarans). Each has been better than the last, but satisfaction is still elusive; there is much yet to be learned. During those decades my early interest expanded with wide reading, considerable travel in the Pacific during World War II and later as a Navy consultant, and then teaching of courses on the geography and ethnology of Oceania, culminating in the last decade with a graduate seminar. Problems concerning the origins and dispersals of the Pacific islanders, and the different kinds of craft they used, have been of much interest. This book results from an attempt to solve one of those problems.

The many people who have helped in one way or another over the years to further this combined interest in Oceanic canoes and their modern equivalents cannot all be cited without my indulging in lengthy autobiography. I will come close enough to that just to mention the more memorable ones.

Although the list could be extended, three former professors influenced me in ways which led at least partially to this book. In the thirties Fred Kniffen gave me an exciting start with tales of sailing on the Great Lakes and with fascinating courses in geography and cultural anthropology. In the early forties R. J. Russell was the best model I have ever encountered of the succinct but lucid presentation of difficult scientific ideas in language which any graduate student could understand. Toward the end of the forties Carl

Sauer inspired me, in courses and seminars, with a vision of how exciting the study of culture history could be. That vision, although attenuated by time and modified by thirty years of contacts with other ideas, is reflected in the pages which follow.

During my nineteen years of tenure, Texas A&M University was a generous home and gave me opportunity to pursue research studies in the culture history of primitive watercraft. Grants on several occasions allowed me to work in the Caribbean and the Pacific, particularly in 1970 when Texas A&M and the American Philosophical Society made possible studies of double-outrigger canoes in the Philippines, rafts in Taiwan, and single outriggers in Micronesia. In those years the Department of Geography and its faculty provided a congenial and inspiring environment.

During the last decade my knowledge of boats was expanded significantly by discourse in my seminar on watercraft. Forty-two research papers by bright and hardworking graduate students have provided much of the background against which this book has been seen in perspective. I can't name them all, so all shall be nameless, but half a dozen studies of Chinese craft, several on Oceania, others on Indian Ocean boats, and a miscellany on various sorts of rafts

and boats from all over the world have taught me much.

Three specific scholarly debts must be acknowledged. George Carter read an early version of the manuscript and made many useful suggestions. Ben Finney made it possible for me to sail on the *Nalehia* and the *Hokule'a*, and from that experience ensued a far better understanding of double canoes. Harry Morss, who read the chapter on seaworthiness, gave his usual friendly but totally candid opinion on its contents; he is not to be blamed for mistakes which remain.

Mention also must be made of the Amateur Yacht Research Society. To the extent that I have it, insight into the sailing characteristics of Pacific canoes comes in great measure from membership for more than twenty years in an uninhibited group which has led the way in the development of modern catamarans and trimarans.

Despite Webb's remarks about *some* authors' wives, I want to conclude by acknowledging more than forty years of unstinting support by Gin. She has carried more than her fair share of all burdens and has done so with grace and with humor. I could have worked on boats without her, but it wouldn't have been nearly so much fun.

EDWIN DORAN

College Station, Texas
June 19, 1980

Acknowledgments for Illustrations

SINCERE thanks is hereby expressed to several individuals and institutions noted below for permission to reprint drawings, maps, or photographs. Sources of other materials which have been redrawn also are acknowledged. Full citations are given in the bibliography. All other illustrations are original to this book.

Fig. 1. Redrawn from Bellwood, 1975, p. 10.

Fig. 2. Reprinted from Davidson, 1935, pp. 79, 80, 82, by permission of the *Journal of the Polynesian Society*.

Fig. 3. Redrawn from Hornell, 1936, p. 332.

Fig. 5. Reprinted by permission of the Polynesian Voyaging Society, and with thanks to Will Kyselke, astronomer.

Figs. 6, 7. Reprinted from Finney, 1977, figs. 2 and 3. Copyright 1977 by the American Association for the Advancement of Science. Also by permission of Ben Finney.

Fig. 8. *Above*, reprinted from Hornell, 1936, fig. 61, by permission of the Bishop Museum Press; *below*, reprinted from Great Britain, Admiralty, 1944b, fig. 203.

Figs. 9–12. Reprinted from Doran, 1972, pp. 144–154, by permission of the *Journal of the Polynesian Society*.

Fig. 13. Reprinted from *Geosciences and Man* 12 (1975): 87, Fig. 4.

Fig. 14. Reprinted from Hornell, 1936, fig. 76, by permission of the Bishop Museum Press.

Figs. 15–17. Reprinted from Doran, 1972, pp. 144–154, by permission of the *Journal of the Polynesian Society*.

Fig. 18. Reprinted from Great Britain, Admiralty, 1944b, figs. 108, 63, and 56.

Fig. 21. Redrawn from sources: A—Jordan, 1979, p. 148; B—Neyret, 1970, p. 5; C—Hornell, 1936, p. 115; D—Hornell, 1936, p. 35; E—Doran, forthcoming; F—Hornell, 1936, p. 379; G—Forrest, 1780, p. 150; H—Remote Area Conflict Information Center, 1967b, p. 260; I—Remote Area Conflict Information Center, 1967a, p. 43.

Fig. 23. After a drawing by Hodges (1774?) by permission of the Mitchell Library, Sydney. Reprinted from Dodd, 1972, p. 77, by permission of Dodd, Mead.

Fig. 24. Reprinted from Haddon, 1937, fig. 96, by permission of the Bishop Museum Press.

Fig. 25. Redrawn from Howells, 1973, pp. 48–49, and from Kroeber, 1948, p. 133.

Fig. 26. Redrawn from Howells, 1973, p. 201.

Fig. 27. Redrawn from Shutler and Marck, 1975, p. 94.

Fig. 28. From Green, 1979, fig. 2.2. Copyright 1979 by the President and Fellows of Harvard College. Reprinted by permission of Harvard University Press.

Fig. 29. Redrawn from Shutler and Marck, 1975, pp. 97, 99.

Fig. 34. Redrawn from Doran, 1972, p. 154, and Finney, 1977, p. 1281.

Fig. 38. Reprinted from Davidson, 1935, p. 80, by permission of the *Journal of the Polynesian Society*.

WANGKA

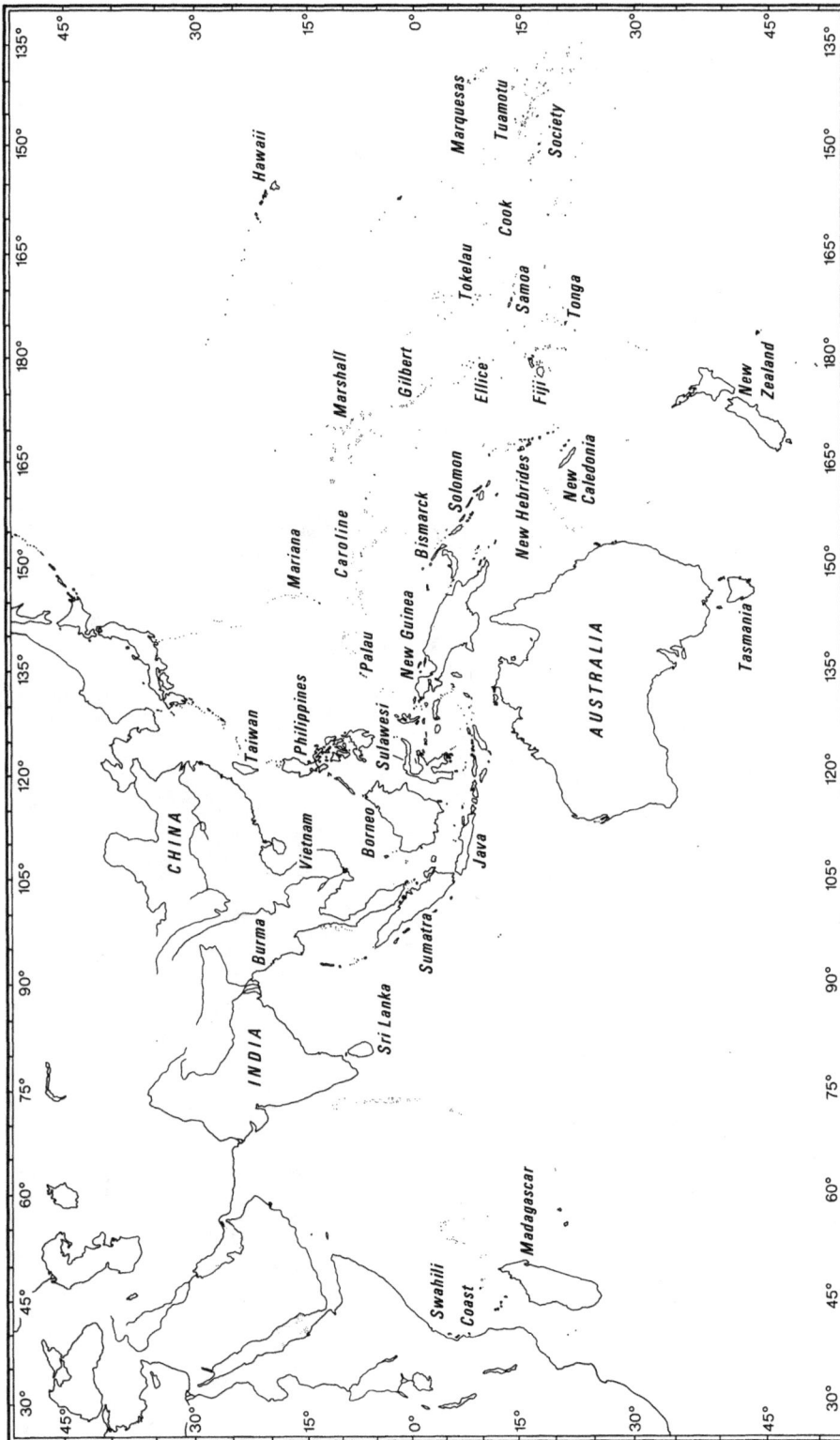

Locations of principal countries, islands, and island groups.

1

Introduction

~~~~~~

THE term *Austronesian* has supplanted an older adjective, *Malayo-Polynesian*, to identify a language phylum spoken by handsome, brown-skinned people across a vast expanse of the Pacific, from Easter Island to Indonesia, and westward to an outlier in Madagascar (Fig. 1). Relatively small cultural differences are recognized by subdivision into areas called Polynesia, Micronesia, Indonesia, Melanesia, and Madagascar, the latter two set off still farther by race mixture dominance by black-skinned, frizzy-haired folk—and in part by languages of several Papuan phyla.

Most Austronesians live on tropical islands large and small surrounded by beautifully transparent water which shades from indigo through turquoise to chartreuse as depth decreases toward snow-white coralline beaches. In the shade of coconut palms or breadfruit trees stand palm-thatched houses, and on or near the beaches are long and narrow canoes, some doubled and others with outriggers on one or both sides. Yams, taro, and sweet potatoes; breadfruit, bananas, and coconuts—these form the basic diet, supplemented rarely by pig, dog, or chicken. But the principal source of protein is the sea. Canoes for fishing are indispensable, and canoes for voyaging to other islands were the means by which the islands of the Pacific were inhabited.

Everywhere Austronesians use names for their canoes which are closely similar. *Wa'a* in Hawaii, *va'a* in Tahiti, *vaka* in Tonga, *wangga* in Fiji, *oanga* between New Britain and New Ireland, *waga* at the eastern tip of New Guinea, *haka* in Banda, *banka* in the Philippines, and *laka* in Madagascar are just a few of the hundreds of cognates. Linguists have reconstructed many words of the Proto-Austronesian language of some three thousand to six thousand years ago, and *wangka* (wäng'-kä) may be the earliest Austronesian word for boat. Canoes are our focus here, and *wangka* symbolizes all Austronesian canoes.

As Westerners discovered the islands from 1500 to 1800 and came to know them better in the last two hundred years, they wondered how and when and whence came people of closely similar speech and culture to be scattered across so vast an expanse of ocean. A century of ethnologic studies and more recent archaeological and linguistic investigations have convinced almost all scholars that Austronesian speakers originated somewhere in Southeast Asia or Indonesia, entered the Pacific perhaps six thousand years ago, and

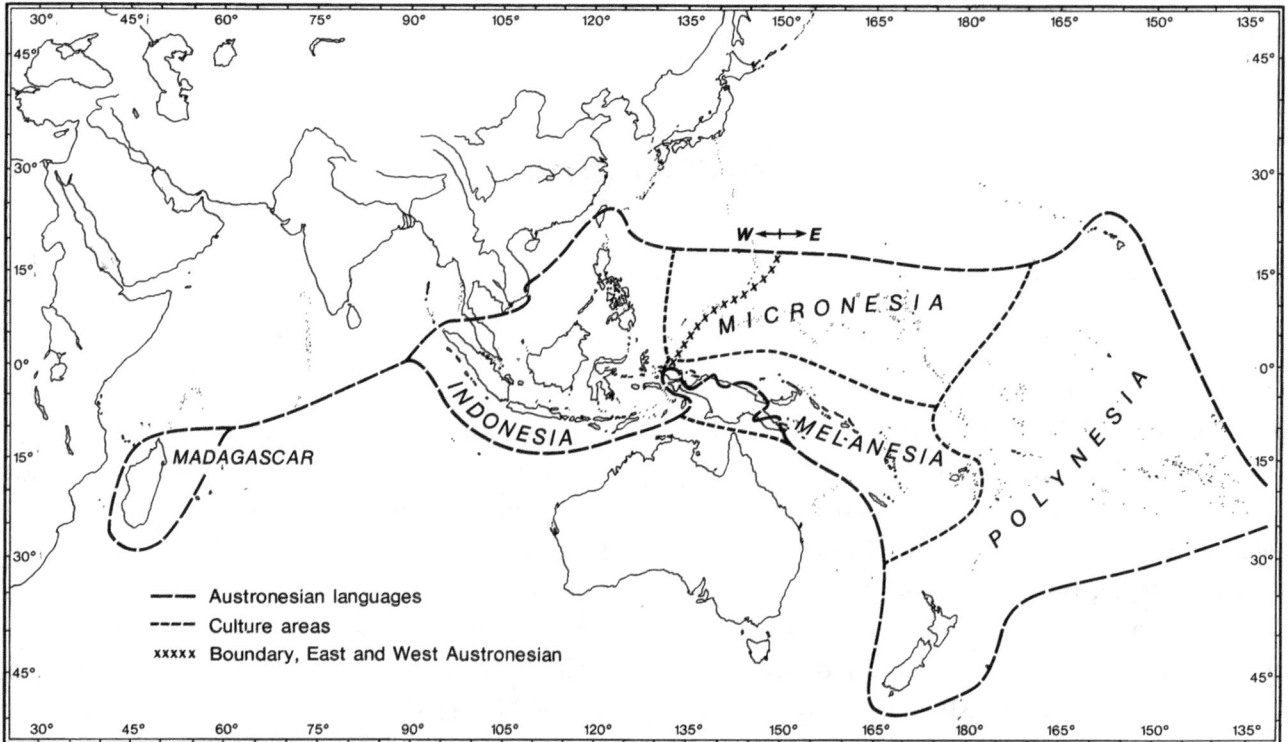

FIG. 1. Austronesian language phylum.

much more recently sailed westward to Madagascar. People ancestral to the Polynesians carried with them their stone tools and horticulture and have maintained them to the present, whereas later traits such as iron tools and rice agriculture flowed into Indonesia as replacements for or additions to the more ancient way of life. In an earlier day, basing their speculations on the distributions of culture traits and plants and using the age-area hypothesis, scientists had already reached these general conclusions which are now vindicated by archaeology and the use of radiocarbon dating and which are, of course, understood far better.

Many questions, however, remain to be an-swered. It is only in the last decade that one basic controversy has been settled and there is general acceptance of the idea that most islands in the Pacific were discovered on controlled voyages of discovery rather than by accidental drifts. A computer simulation of one hundred thousand drift voyages indicates only a minute chance that the extremities of Polynesia could have been settled accidentally, but a simulated ability for canoes to sail with wind at 90° to course permits voyages to any place in the Pacific (Levinson, Ward, and Webb, 1973). Allegations by the drift-voyage school that navigational knowledge of the islanders was inadequate to permit return voyages have been disproved by David Lewis' definitive work

(1972). Finally, a series of studies of Pacific canoe performance has shown that native craft were both strong enough and capable of sailing closely enough to the wind to have accomplished purposeful return voyages (Gladwin, 1970; Doran, 1972, 1975; Finney, 1967, 1977). Other questions are still debated, and it is consideration of one of them which leads to this volume.

Contributions to our knowledge of Austronesian canoes far exceeding those from any other source were made by A. C. Haddon, a British anthropologist, and James Hornell, a British fisheries biologist who became the world authority on primitive watercraft, in a series of papers and books between 1918 and 1946. The descriptive detail which they provide, based on many years of field work from East Africa to easternmost Polynesia and on intensive museum and library study, is the basis for all subsequent work. In final interpretation of their amassed data they conclude that the oldest canoes are double outriggers, followed more or less simultaneously by double canoes and single outriggers (Hornell, 1936; Haddon, 1937; and Haddon and Hornell, 1938;

slightly modified in Hornell, 1946). This book is a respectful, perhaps slightly diffident, dissent.

After examining the most recent developments in physical anthropology, linguistics, and archaeology which bear on the problem, I shall analyze canoe seaworthiness and conclude by examining the distributional evidence in greater detail than that of earlier studies. I hypothesize on the basis of all the facts that double canoes, then single outriggers as used in Polynesia, are the oldest Austronesian boat types, followed by Micronesian and Melanesian single outriggers of different sail type and most recently by Indonesian double-outrigger canoes. The center of complexity of Austronesian boat traits lies in the islands surrounding Sulawesi, and that is probably the center of innovation from which many traits spread outward. It will be noted, however, that the highest development of single-outrigger canoes was reached in Micronesia and that the place of origin of double outriggers was probably Vietnam. Before looking at the evidence, however, we must describe in some detail the craft whose origins and relatives ages are at issue.

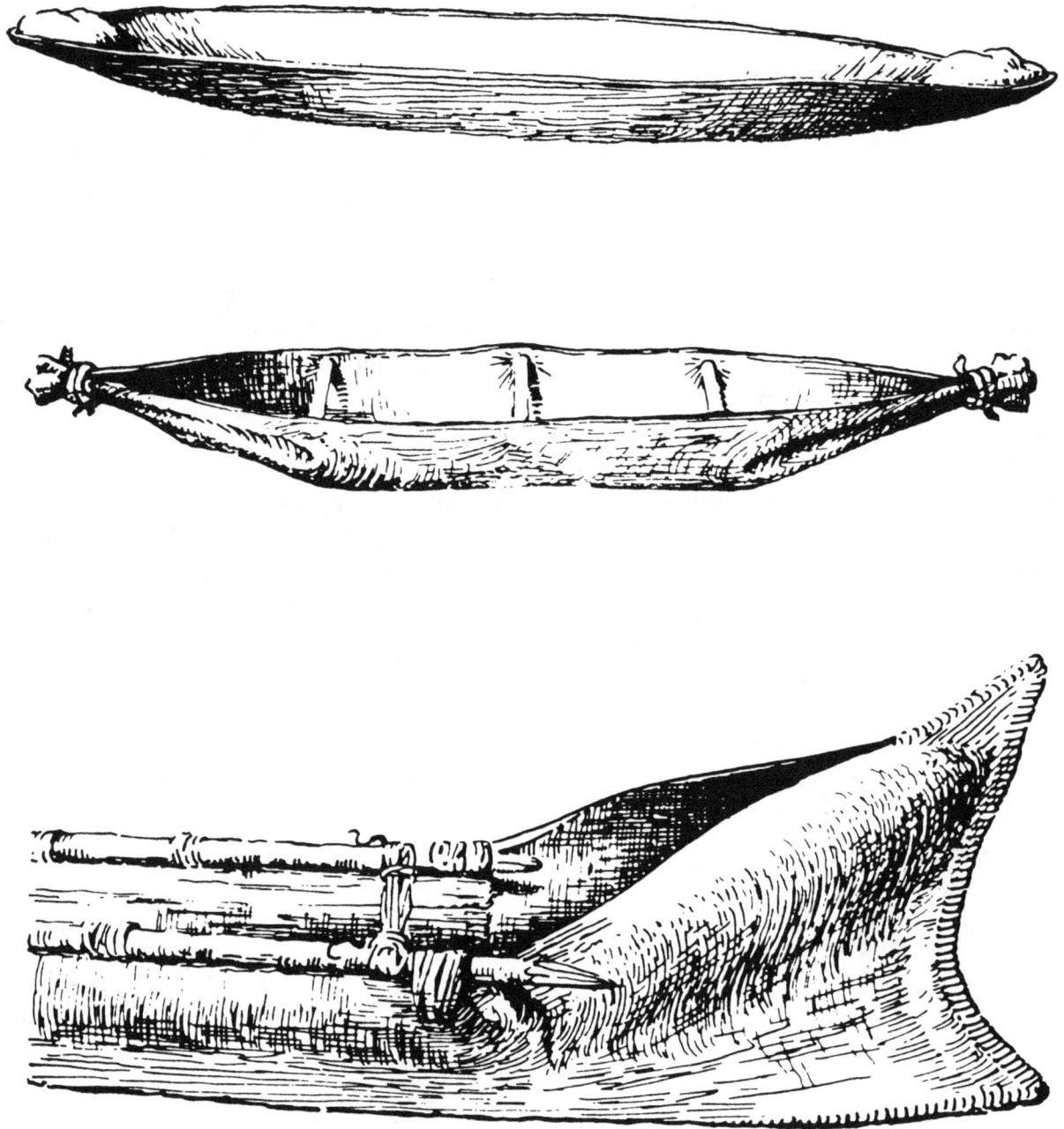

FIG. 2. Three types of Australian bark boats: *top*, simple bark canoe, Victoria and Murray River; *center*, tied bark canoe, east coast of southeastern Australia; and *bottom*, sewn bark canoe, Melville Island type.

2

The Canoes

~~~~~~

VERBAL descriptions of watercraft are difficult to write and to comprehend for several reasons. The craft themselves are complex; a complete description, plank by plank, dimension by dimension, requires many words and submerges the reader in detail. In addition, precise description requires a nautical vocabulary of many dozens of words unlikely to be known to anyone except a few experts. Finally, even the full English nautical vocabulary is inadequate to describe a number of features on Austronesian canoes because their counterparts do not exist on Western craft. For these reasons the sections which follow and describe hull types, sailing techniques, and sail types will be heavily weighted toward photographs and drawings. Nautical vocabulary will be kept to a reasonable minimum, and as few new terms as possible will be invented for adequate description.

HULL TYPES

1. *Bark Boats*. Among the simplest, and presumably most ancient, types of watercraft in Austronesia are boats made of bark. The simplest of all are formed of bark sheets plugged at the ends with clay, whereas others are tied at the ends and more complex ones have sewed ends (Fig. 2). The principal location of bark canoes is Australia, but a few relicts are found in Indonesia, probably indicating a once much wider distribution.

The very simple bark rafts of the Tasmanians allowed some mobility on the water but became waterlogged in about six hours and were never used for distances offshore greater than about eight miles (Jones, 1977, pp. 322–326).

2. *Rafts*. Wood or bamboo rafts are mostly of simple construction—a number of poles lashed side by side to a few cross-poles—and require little by way of description (Fig. 3). They may be more elaborate, shaped with the center log longer than the others or with a stepped arrangement on either side of the centerline. Only in Mangareva, Tonga, and probably Yap were rafts equipped with sails. Elaborate and sophisticated sailing rafts with leeway boards are probably unrelated to and lie beyond the Austronesian area in

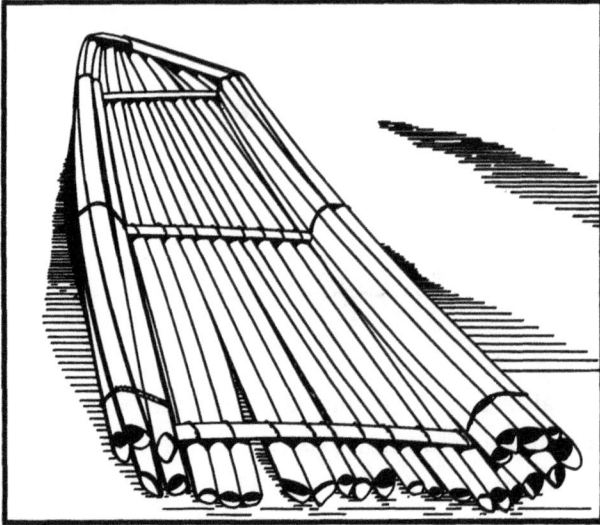

FIG. 3. Fijian bamboo raft.

South India, Vietnam, Formosa, and Ecuador. (See Doran, 1967, on leeboards and Doran, 1971, for a discussion of the sailing raft tradition.)

3. *Dugouts*. Simple shaped and hollowed-out logs, occasionally with a wash strake added to increase freeboard (Fig. 4), are abundant in Austronesia and also require little description, in part because no one has ever studied them. I noticed casually some four or five different subtypes in Sulu alone in 1970, but my attention, like that of most other past observers, was focused on outriggers. Differences and similarities among dugouts and their cultural significance are almost completely unknown.

4. *Double Canoes*. The first of the three principal hull configurations used in Austronesia is constructed by lashing two dugout hulls, almost always with wash strakes added, to cross-booms which separate them by a few feet (the modern analogue is the catamaran). Our knowledge of double canoes is severely limited by the fact that

they disappeared in Polynesia at least a century ago, and we must depend on rather limited descriptions and drawings made in the late eighteenth and early nineteenth centuries. In only one place in Austronesia, the Mailu area of southeastern Papua, are double canoes in existence still; a double canoe from that area was seen in the nearby Amphlett Islands in the late 1960's (Lauer, 1970, p. 392), and anthropologists sailed on double canoes in 1973 (Allen, 1979).

A modern double canoe, the *Hokule'a*, was tested in Hawaiian waters in 1975 and 1976 and then sailed to Tahiti and back in 1976 (Figs. 5 and 6; see Finney, 1977, 1979*a*, and 1979*b* for detailed descriptions of construction and sailing of the *Hokule'a* and for scientific results). Although modern materials were used in its construction, and Hawaiianlike topsides are superimposed on a Tahitian or Tuamotuan hull shape, all critical parts of the *Hokule'a*'s design are based on known Polynesian precedents. Its sailing performance is probably about the same as that of authentic canoes of a millennium past, and much has been learned from observations made on the canoe in Hawaii and during its round trip to Tahiti. More accurate, because it is based on plans measured in Hawaii by Admiral Paris in 1839, is another facsimile, the *Nalehia* (Fig. 7; Finney, 1977). Paddling experiments conducted by Finney in the *Nalehia* indicate a high degree of improbability that such long-distance voyages as that from Tahiti to Hawaii could have been made except by use of sails (Horvath and Finney, 1976).

Two other double canoes, one seen in the Tuamotus about 1840 and a plan view of an *orou* from Mailu, illustrate characteristics which are subtly different from those typical in Polynesia

FIG. 4. Large dugout near Bongao, Sulu Archipelago.

FIG. 5. Modern double canoe analogue *Hokule'a*.

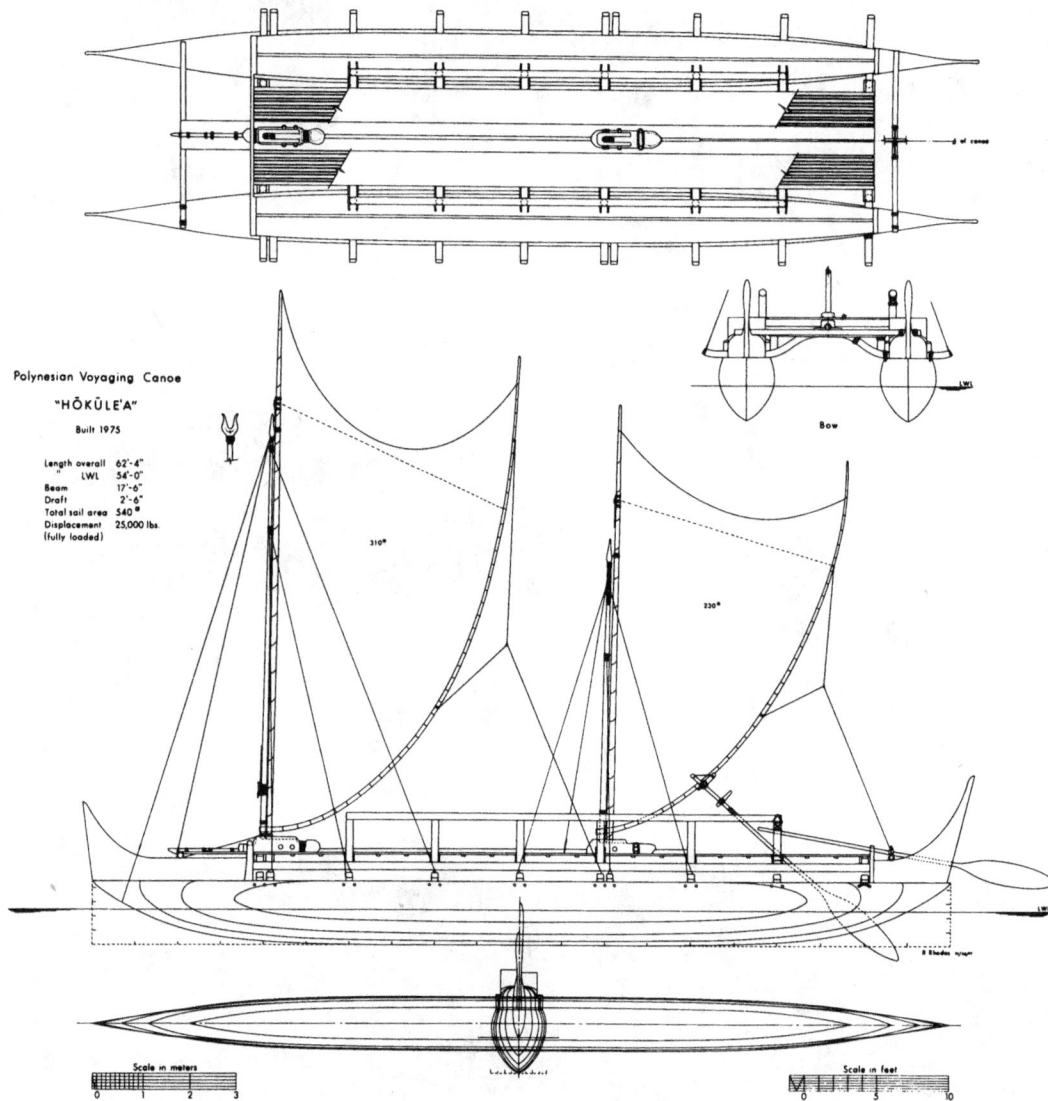

FIG. 6. Sail and deck plans, end views, and lines of *Hokule'a*.

Hawaiian Sailing Canoe
"NALEHIA"
Built 1966

Length overall 42'-2½"
"   LWL   37'-9"
Beam   7'-5"
Draft   1'-1½"

Bow

Stern

Scale in meters

Scale in feet

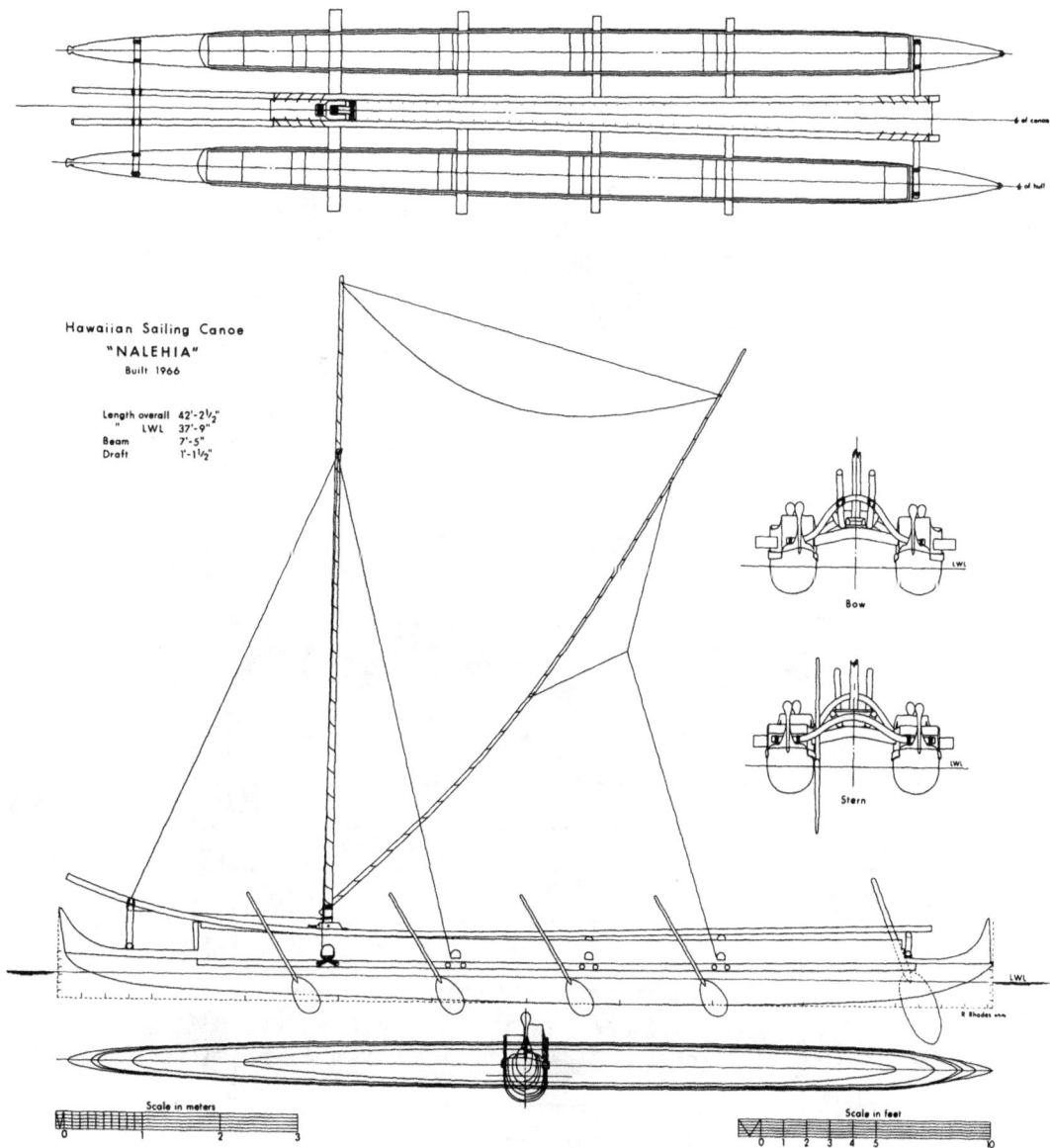

FIG. 7. Sail and deck plans, end views, and lines of *Nalehia*.

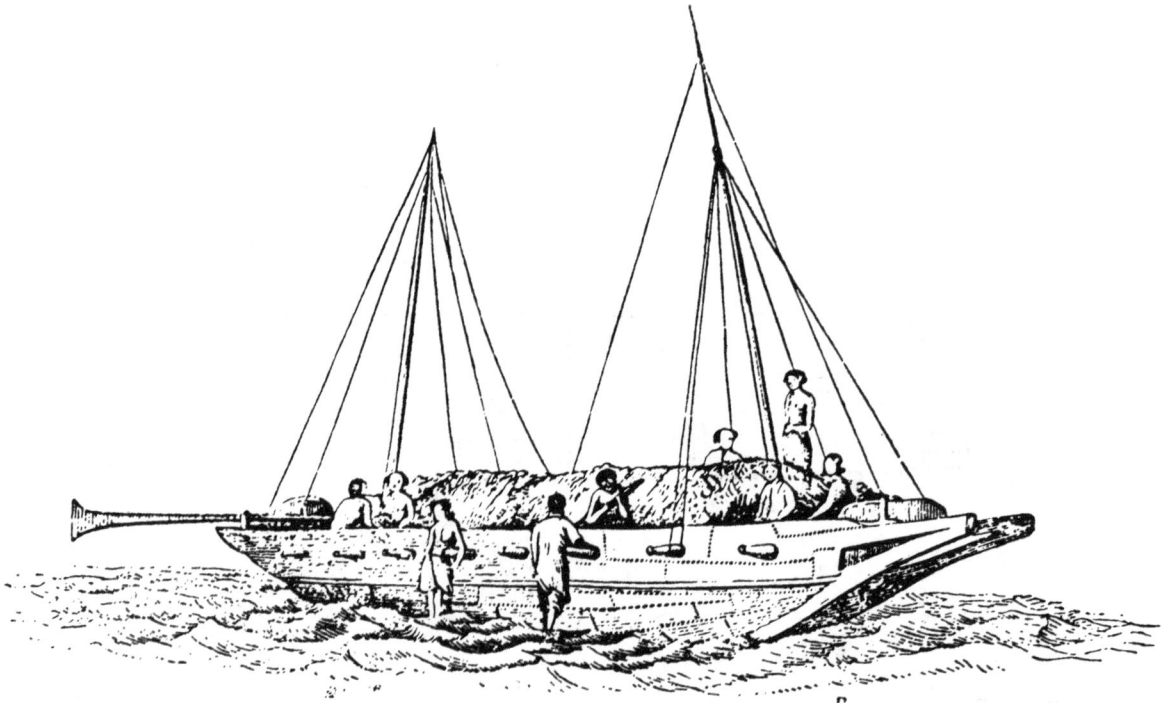

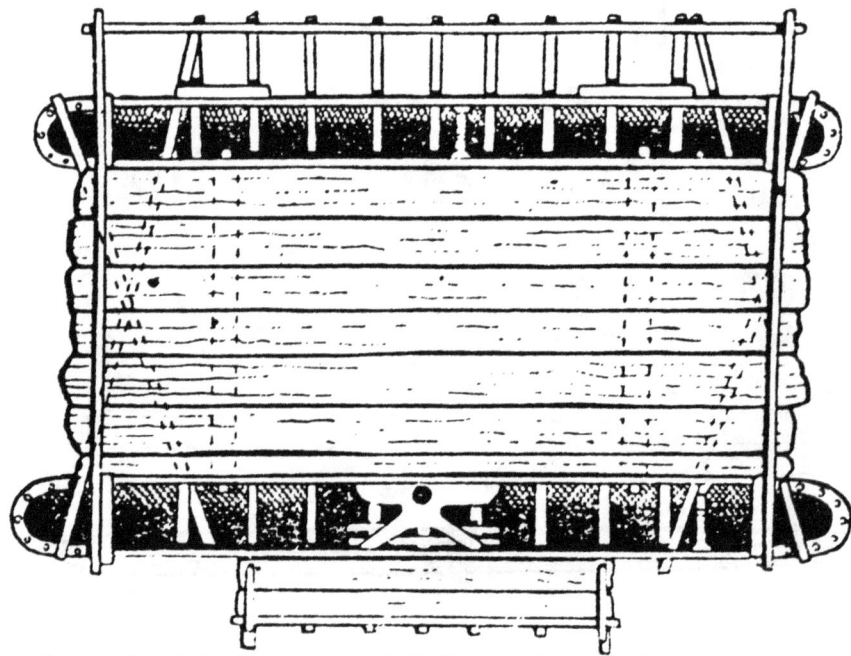

FIG. 8. Double canoes from (*above*) the Tuamotus and (*below*) Mailu, New Guinea.

FIG. 9. The single-outrigger *wa* of Puluwat Atoll.

(Fig. 8). The tiny but critical differences in form have to do with their symmetry. All Western watercraft and the canoes of Figs. 6 and 7 are bilaterally symmetrical across a vertical plane which extends fore and aft along the centerline. In other words, the right and left sides of the boats are mirror images. The canoes of Fig. 8, in contrast, are bilaterally symmetrical across a plane which extends athwartships (side to side) through the middle. In the latter case the two *ends* of the craft are mirror images. These differences in design follow directly from different techniques by which the craft are sailed (to be discussed later) and in turn provide useful clues toward work-ing out the culture history of Austronesian watercraft.

5. *Single-Outrigger Canoes.* As the name implies, stability is provided in these canoes by a single float which is boomed out to one side (Fig. 9). (Their modern analogue, the proa, is rarely seen.) On the sail plan of a typical Micronesian single-outrigger canoe (Fig. 10) it can be noted that the center of effort of the sail (*CE*) is well forward of amidships, a feature to which we shall refer later in considering sail balance. The plan view (Fig. 11) shows the strong diagonal bracing of the main outrigger beams and the platform on the lee side used in maintaining balance. Lines

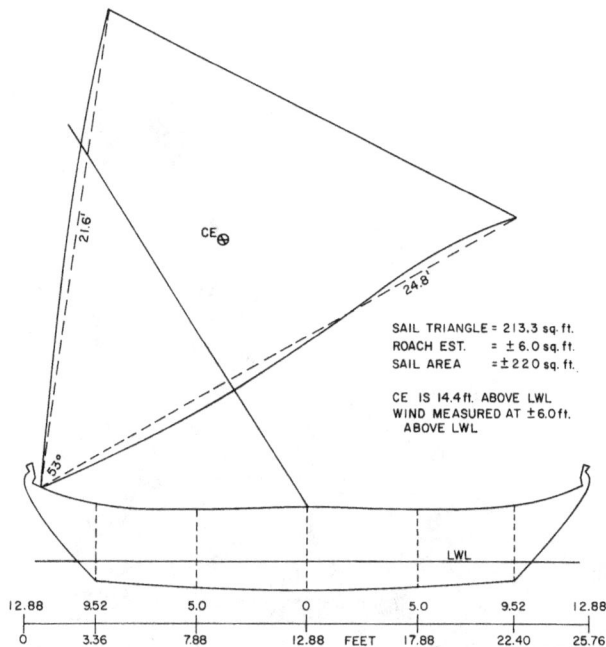

SAIL TRIANGLE = 213.3 sq.ft.
ROACH EST.   = ± 6.0 sq.ft.
SAIL AREA   = ± 220 sq.ft.

CE IS 14.4 ft. ABOVE LWL
WIND MEASURED AT ± 6.0 ft.
ABOVE LWL

| 12.88 | 9.52 | 5.0 | 0 | 5.0 | 9.52 | 12.88 |
| 0 | 3.36 | 7.88 | 12.88 FEET | 17.88 | 22.40 | 25.76 |

Fig. 10. Sail plan of the *wa Mikael*.

drawings of a fast canoe (Fig. 12) and a slow canoe (Fig. 13) from the same atoll (Puluwat) demonstrate the general shape of the canoe hulls (note asymmetry in the end views) but also show details (smooth curves or fairing and sharper entry at the waterline) which cause the differences in the two canoes' speeds.

Another single-outrigger canoe, similar in general form but with certain critical differences from the Micronesian canoes, was sketched in Tahiti about 150 years ago (Fig. 14). The sail area is farther aft, the sail is of different type (discussed later), and the bow end is quite different from the stern end.

Because of the float on only one side, no single-outrigger canoe can be bilaterally symmetrical across a fore-and-aft plane (that is, its right and left sides cannot be mirror images), but the Puluwat canoes (and all other Micronesian and many Melanesian single outriggers) are end-symmetri-

cal across a thwartships plane. Tahitian canoes (and most Polynesian canoes) are totally asymmetrical. As in the case of double canoes, these hull symmetries will tell us something about sailing techniques and in turn about the canoes' historical development.

6. *Double-Outrigger Canoes*. A central hull with floats extended to both sides by cross-booms characterizes the sixth and last Austronesian hull type. (Its modern analogue is the trimaran.) A typical Sulu Archipelago *vinta* shows a good turn of speed with wind from the beam (broadside), crew hiking to windward, and lee float almost burying (Fig. 15). Note that the float on the windward side does not touch the water, a posture typical of all double-outrigger canoes; stability is derived from the buoyancy of the lee float plus the weight of the weather float. The sail plan demonstrates that the mast is well forward but the center of effort about amidships (Fig. 16). The plan and lines views of the same *vinta* (Fig. 17) present the general double-outrigger canoe configuration, floats out to both sides, and also some of the distinctive characteristics which set the *vinta* off as a particular type (unusual cross-boom braces and the squared-off bottom of the dugout hull).

For comparison, other double-outrigger types from Indonesia are illustrated in Fig. 18. The large canoes from Sulawesi and Bali (Fig. 18, *top* and *lower left*) use the same sail type as that of the Sulu canoe but have different techniques of attachment of the floats to the cross-booms. The little fishing canoe from East Java (Fig. 18, *lower right*) is the simplest of all and has a different sail type.

SPLASH RAIL

GUNWALE

DOTTED AREA IS LOAD-CARRYING
SURFACE OF HELMSMAN'S BENCH
AND LEE PLATFORM; 1.5 FEET
HIGHER THAN GUNWALES

GUNWALE

SPLASH RAIL

MAST
STEP

PLANK

PLANK

LOCATION & SIZE OF THE
EIGHT THWARTS ESTIMATED
FROM PHOTOGRAPH

LWL

| 12.88 | 9.52 | 5.0 | 0 | 5.0 | 9.52 | 12.88 |
| 0 | 3.36 | 7.88 | 12.88 FEET | 17.88 | 22.40 | 25.76 |

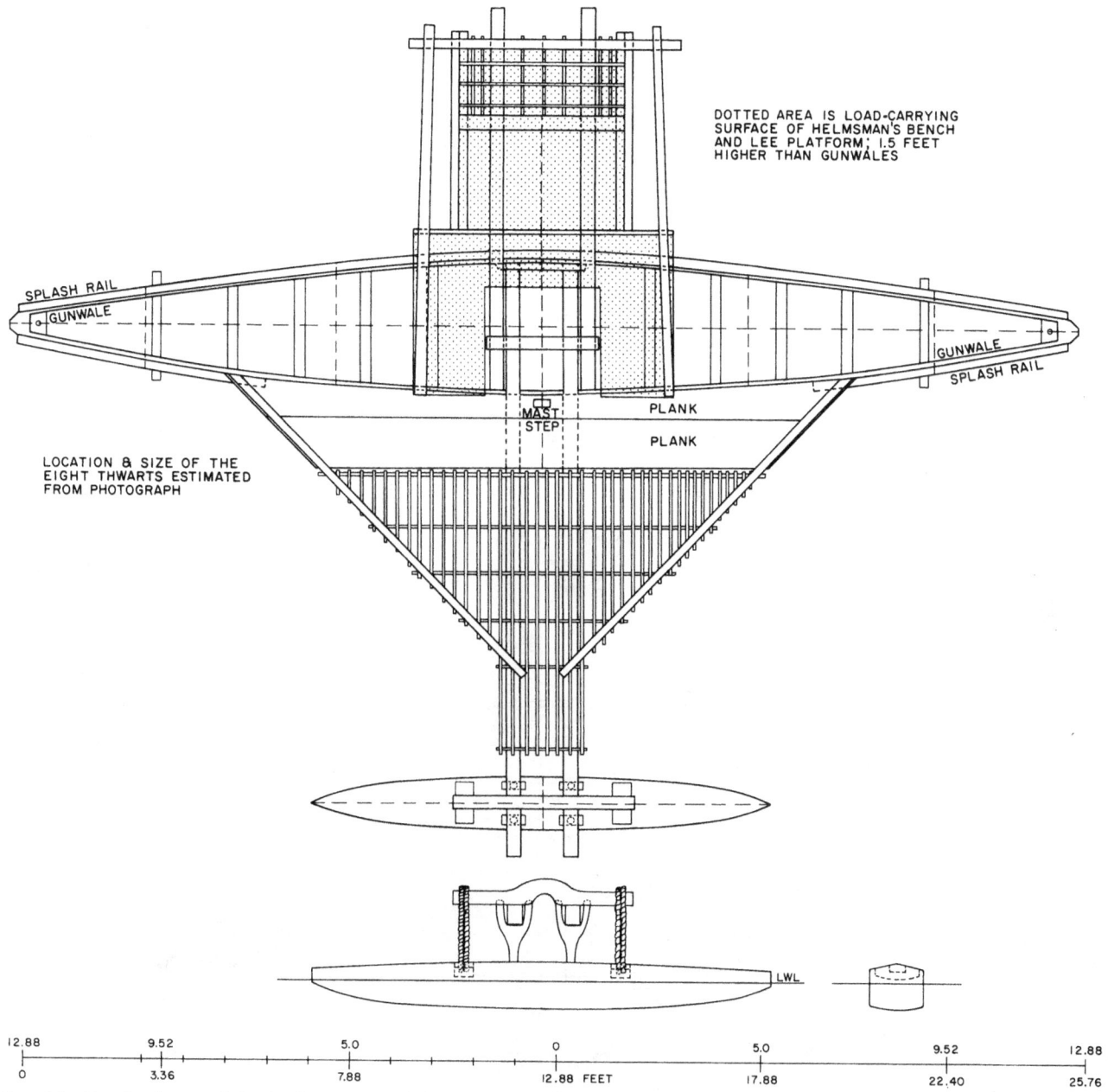

FIG. 11. Deck plan and float elevations of the *wa Mikael*.

SHEER PLAN OF LEE SIDE

WL 2
WL 1
LWL
BUT 1
WL -1

CHINES ARE SHOWN AS DOTTED LINES

GUNWALE
LWL
WL -1
LEE BUT 1
LEE
WEATHER

FULL-BREADTH PLAN

| 12.88 | 9.52 | 5.0 | 0 | 5.0 | 9.52 | 12.88 |
| 0 | 3.36 | 7.88 | 12.88 FEET | 17.88 | 22.40 | 25.76 |

HELMSMAN'S BENCH   LEE PLATFORM

WEATHER   LEE

WEATHER   LEE

LWL

LWL

END ELEVATION,
NOT A BODY PLAN

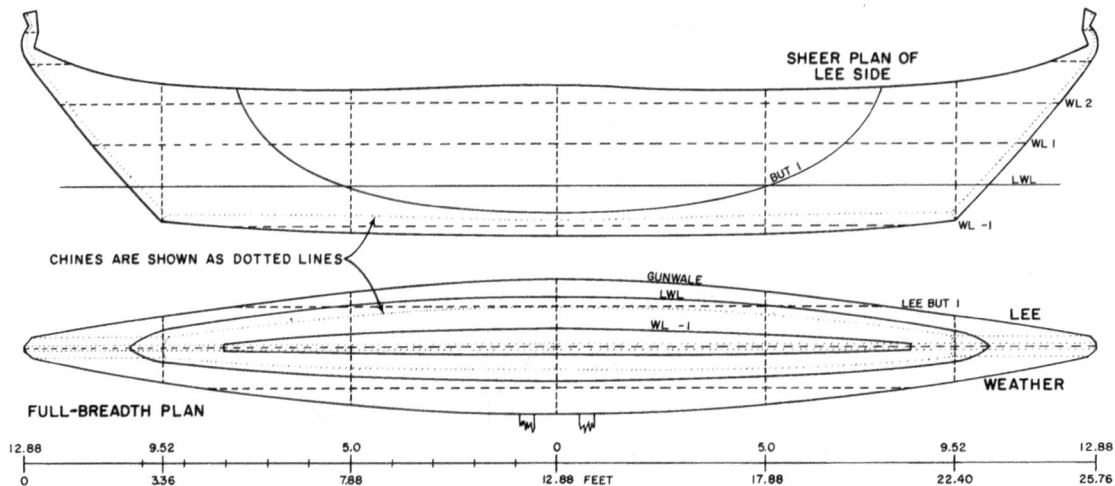

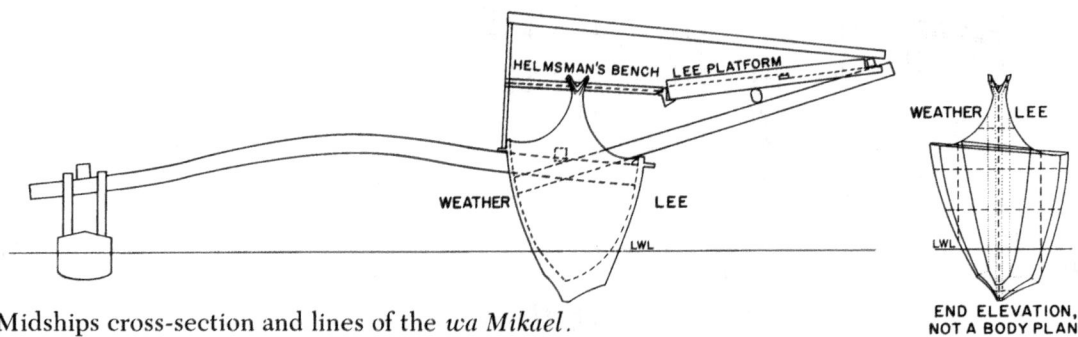

FIG. 12. Midships cross-section and lines of the *wa Mikael*.

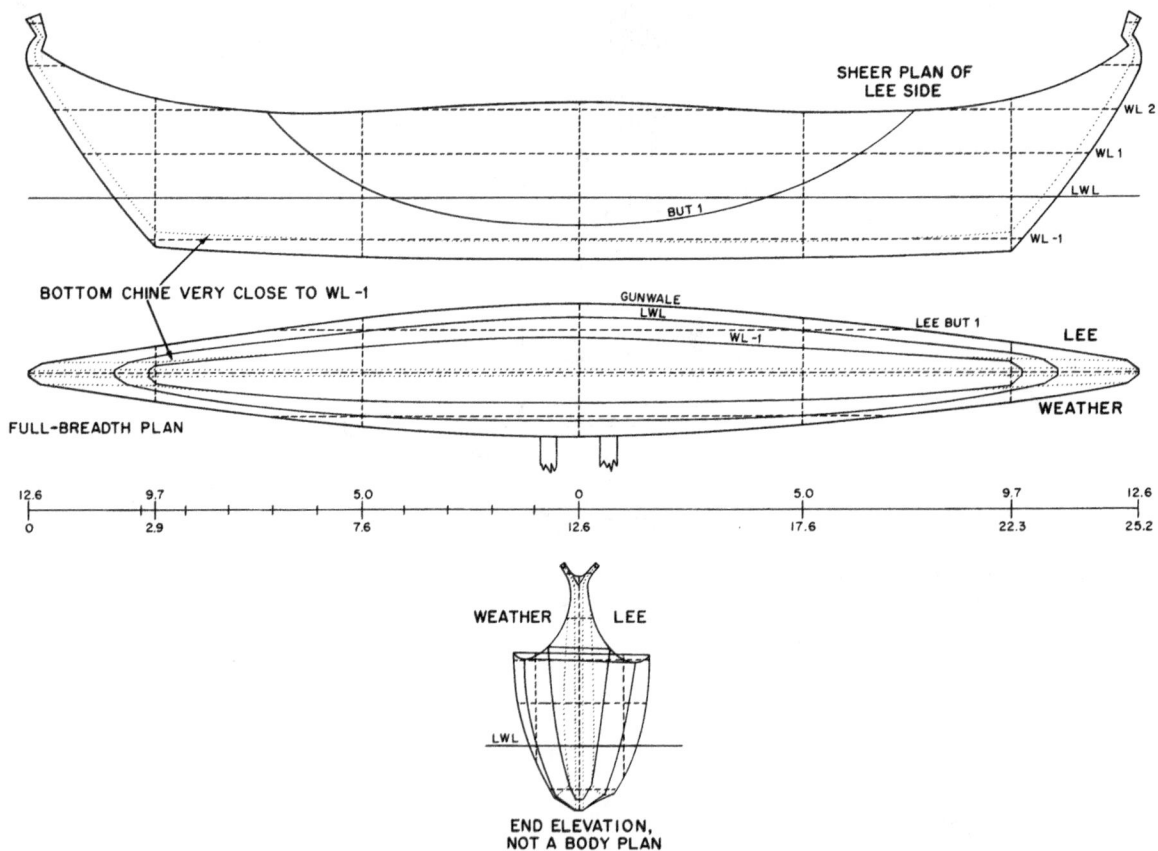

SHEER PLAN OF LEE SIDE

WL 2
WL 1
LWL
BUT 1
WL -1

BOTTOM CHINE VERY CLOSE TO WL -1

GUNWALE
LWL
WL -1
LEE BUT 1
LEE
WEATHER

FULL-BREADTH PLAN

| 12.6 | 9.7 | 5.0 | 0 | 5.0 | 9.7 | 12.6 |
| 0 | 2.9 | 7.6 | 12.6 | 17.6 | 22.3 | 25.2 |

WEATHER   LEE

LWL

END ELEVATION,
NOT A BODY PLAN

FIG. 13. Hull lines of *Epifano*, another Puluwat canoe.

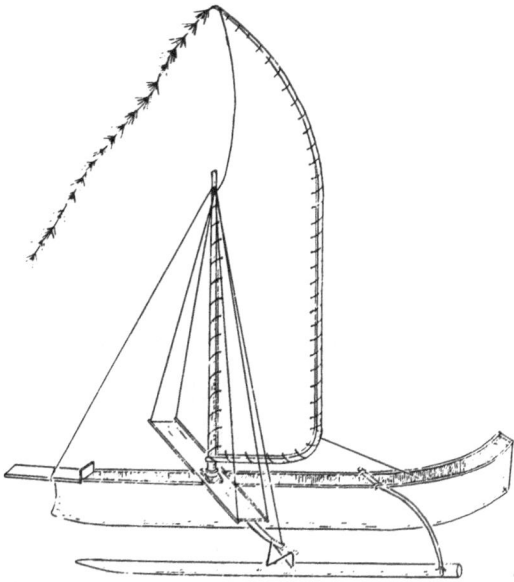

FIG. 14. Single-outrigger canoe from Tahiti.

FIG. 15. The *vinta Nardi* off Bongao, Sulu.

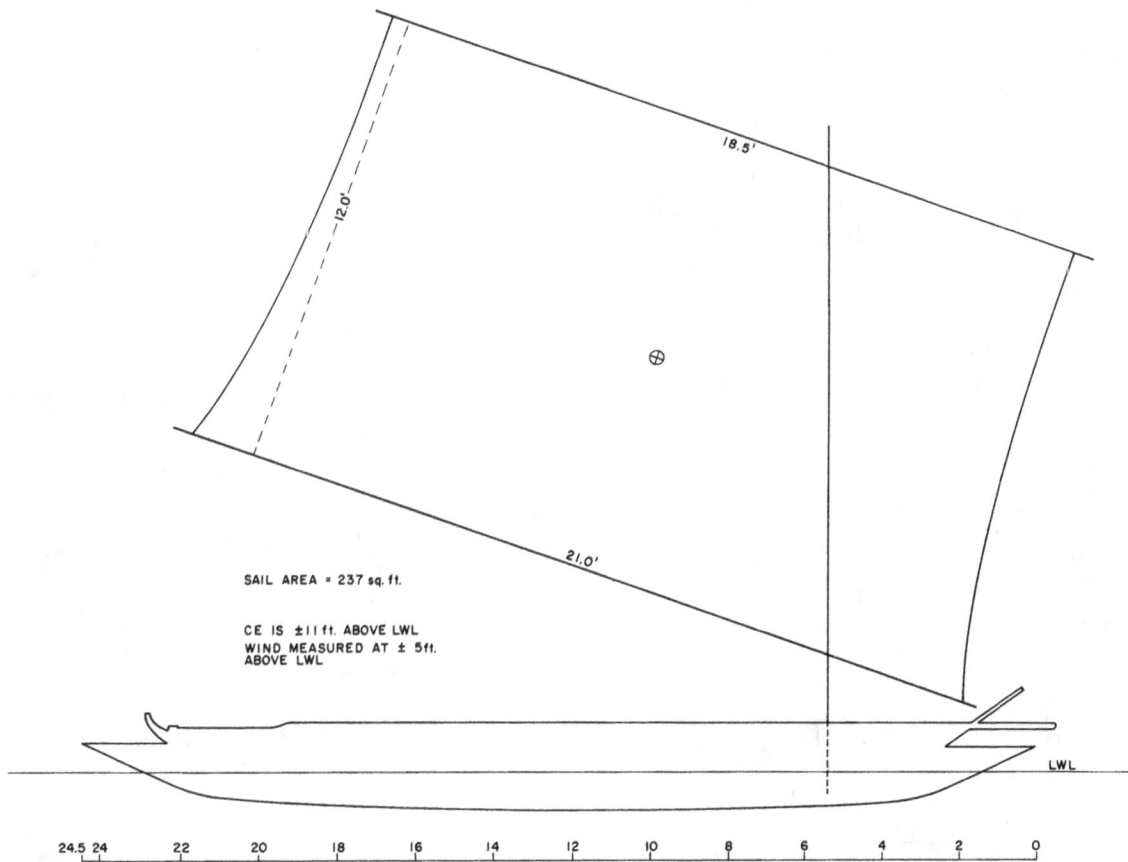

SAIL AREA = 237 sq. ft.

CE IS ±11 ft. ABOVE LWL
WIND MEASURED AT ± 5ft.
ABOVE LWL

FIG. 16. Sail plan of the *vinta Nardi*.

Wangka

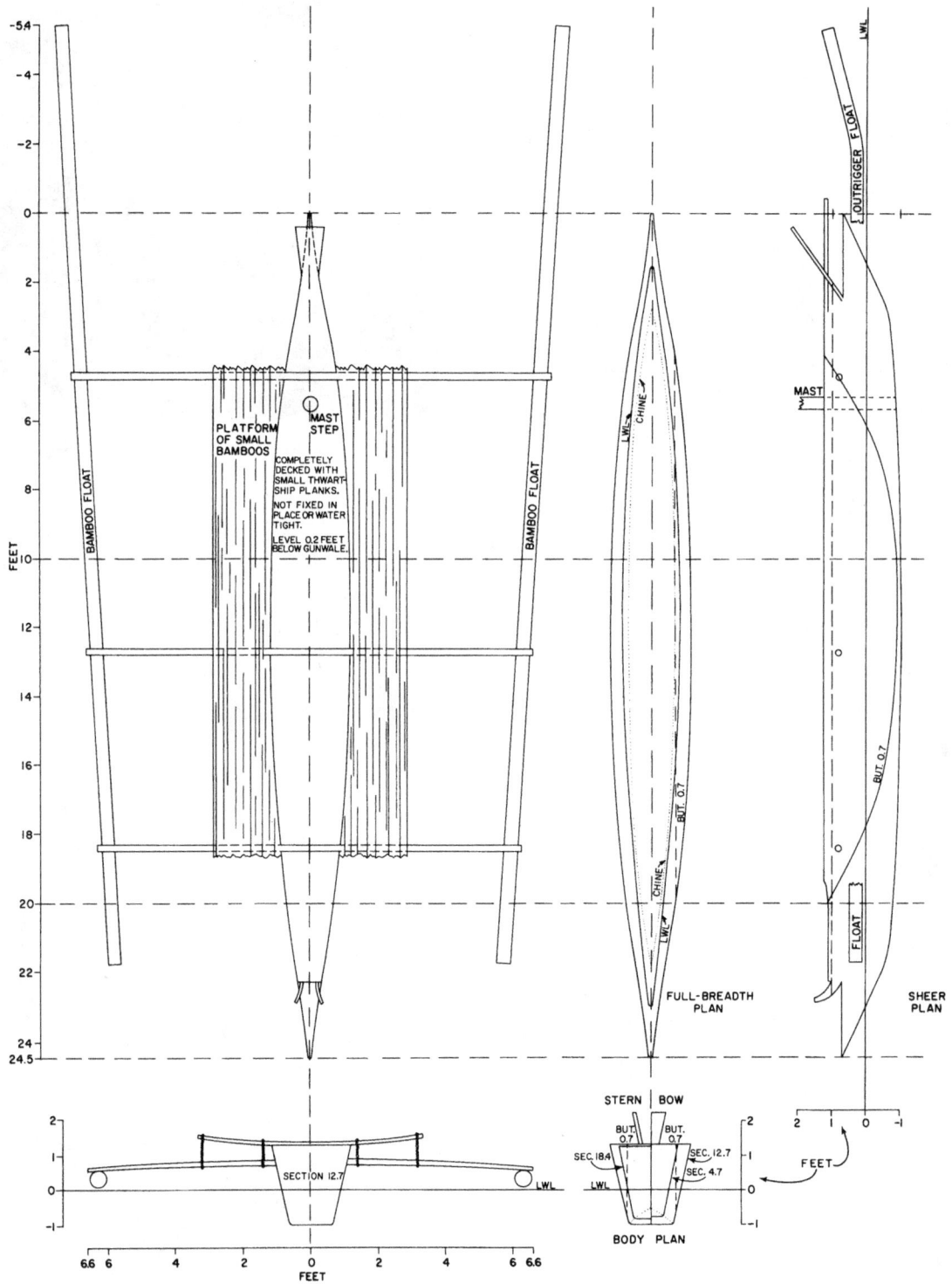

FIG. 17. Plan, midships section, and lines of the *vinta Nardi*.

Fɪɢ. 18. Double-outrigger canoes from (*top*) Sulawesi, (*bottom left*) Bali, and (*bottom right*) East Java.

TACKING AND SHUNTING TECHNIQUES

Although it is physically impossible for a sailing craft to make progress directly against the wind, all Austronesian sailing canoes can make good a course about 60° to 65° off the true wind, and some are better. (For comparison, square-riggers of the nineteenth century could make good about 67° off the true wind, and most modern sailing yachts can make good 45° (see Fig. 19). By sailing a zig-zag course, canoes can eventually make good a course directly to windward. Many Austronesian canoes (and practically all Western craft) change from "zig" to "zag" by the maneuver called tacking (Fig. 20A). The canoe sails along (1) and at an appropriate point (2) heads into the wind. Momentum carries the boat forward as it completes the turn, the sail fills on the opposite side, and the canoe sails off on the new tack (3). The outrigger float which earlier was on the windward side (1) is on the lee side (3) on the new tack. The well-known procedure is described in detail only for comparison with a quite different technique, used uniquely in parts of the Pacific and Indian oceans, which is called "shunting."*

We shall examine the critical matter of canoe stability in detail later, but for the moment let us accept the fact that a canoe sailing with float to leeward is difficult to handle because the float tends to submerge and produce a capsize. If the float can be kept always to weather, ideally just skimming the water surface, the chance of capsize is somewhat lower and the canoe speed is much improved. For these reasons the technique of shunting was invented somewhere in Austronesia. As Fig. 20B shows, a canoe sailing with float to weather (1) sheets in a bit, that is, hauls the sail in (2), causing the canoe to bear off with wind abeam (3). As soon as this position is reached, the sheet is completely slacked (3a), and the entire sail rig is shifted to the opposite end of the boat (3b, 3c). The sail is then sheeted in (3d), and the canoe begins to move off on the new tack (4). What appears to a Westerner as total chaos is actually a superbly coordinated maneuver which takes less time to perform than it takes to read this paragraph. The former stern has become the bow, and the float has remained in the desired position to weather of the main hull.

---

* Although David Lewis and Ben Finney have given me credit for devising this application of the word *shunting* (Lewis, 1978, p. 52; Finney, 1979b, p. 326), it has been used in this way for several years by members of the Amateur Yacht Research Society (see *AYRS Airs*, 1972), probably first by Dr. John Morwood, the organization's founder and editor at that time.

Course sailed
(heading)

Course made good

True
Wind

Angle made
good off the
true wind

Leeway angle

True
Wind

1.0

To make good one unit of distance against the true wind
these distances must be sailed :

Yacht   1.4
Canoe   2.0
Square Rigger   2.6

DISTANCE AGAINST TRUE WIND

Yacht

Pacific Canoe

Square Rigger

67°
60°
45°

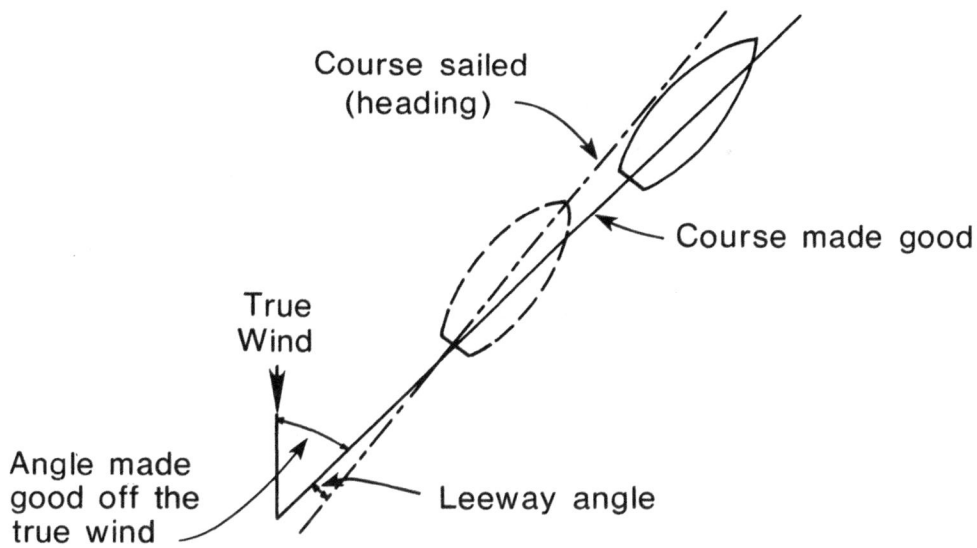

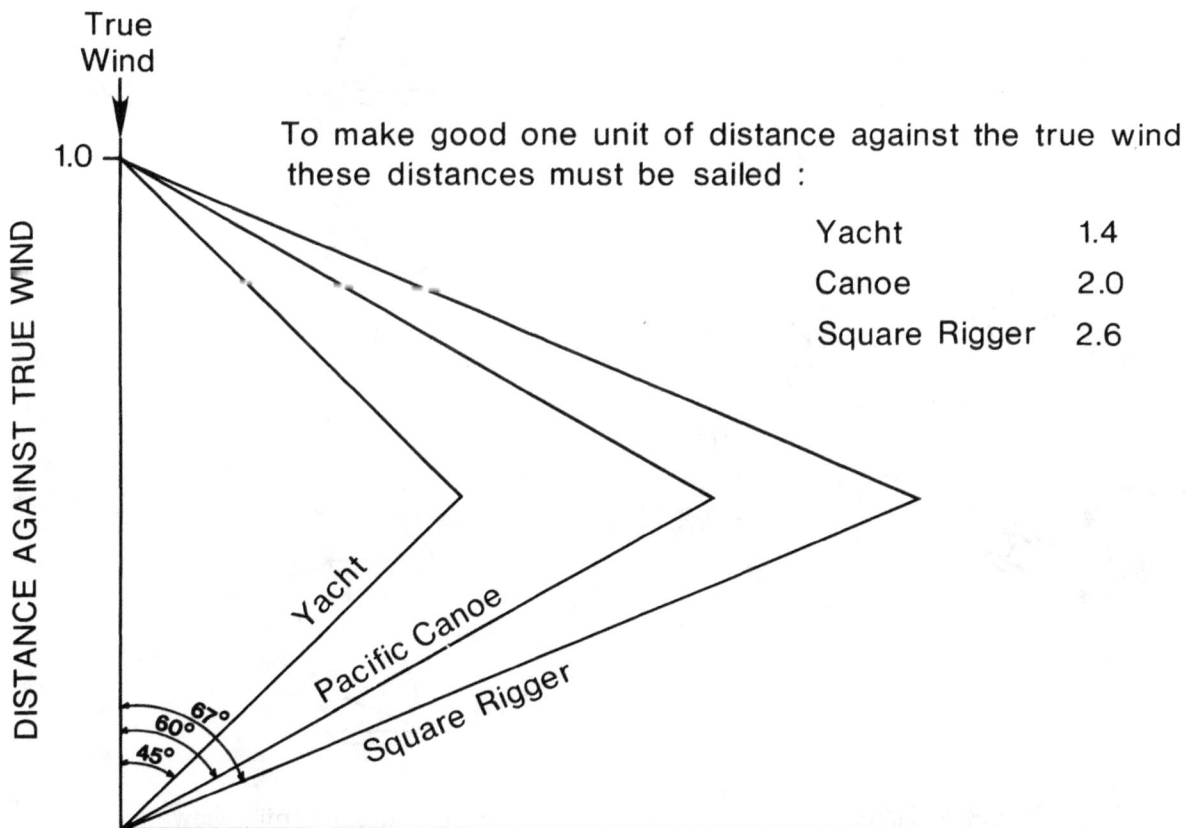

FIG. 19. Diagrams illustrating (*above*) angle made good off the true wind and (*below*) distance made good.

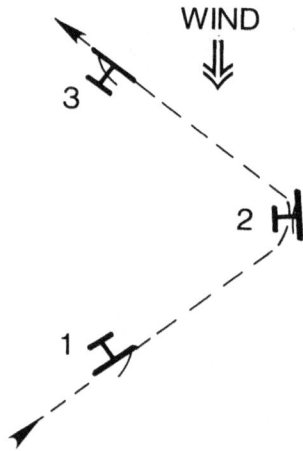

A. TACKING

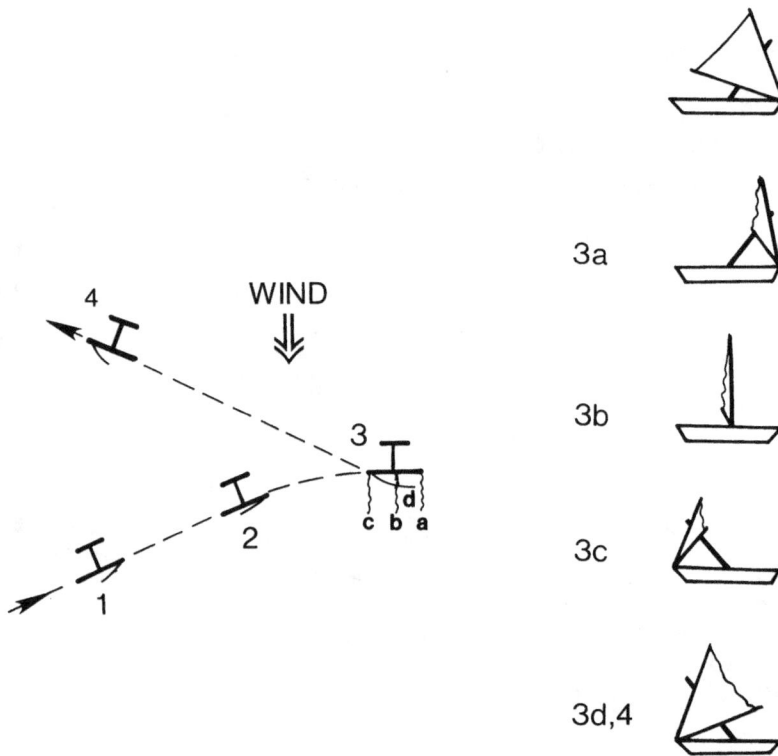

B. SHUNTING

Boat and sail profile viewed from lee side.

FIG. 20. Techniques of *A*, tacking, and *B*, shunting.

SAIL TYPES

If difficulty has been encountered with a sailing maneuver which was unknown in the West, it is small compared to the problems of recognition and nomenclature involving Austronesian sails. I shall consider a sail type to exist if it is so distinctively different from other types that most informed students recognize it as a separate type and if the type is found in a conterminous area of appreciable size. Unusual sails, found in small numbers at widely separated points, are probably aberrant and do not warrant recognition as types. In selecting names, two guiding principles also will be followed: where sails or parts of sails are clearly analogous to those same sails or parts in the West, the Western nautical terminology will be used, and where unambiguous names have been applied in the past, historical precedence will rule. If neither principle can be followed, it will be necessary to apply a new name.

The traditional Western sail for five thousand years (described for contrast) is a "square" sail which is rigged athwartships and used in such fashion that the wind blows always against the same side of the sail. Austronesian sails (and of course many late Western sails, including those of modern yachts) are "fore-and-aft" sails which will flutter more or less gently in a vertical fore-and-aft plane when the canoe is headed directly into the wind. On alternate tacks the wind blows against alternate sides of the sail. Standard vocabulary again allows us to subdivide Austronesian fore-and-aft sails into two categories: spritsails and lugsails. Spritsails are supported on two spars which are close together or touching at the lower end and divergent to two sail corners aloft (Fig.

21, the first six sails). Lugsails are attached along the upper edge to a yard which is hoisted aloft on a mast in such manner that a smaller part of the sail is forward of the mast and most of the sail area is aft of the mast (Fig. 21, last three sails). Omitted from all nine sketches are the complexly varying stays, shrouds, or vangs which steady the spars or permit their manipulation.

The simple problems of recognition and nomenclature are now past as we turn to examination of the nine most important Austronesian sail types. The letters identifying each type refer to the letters in Fig. 21.

A. Double Spritsail. Found at present in only a few locations around the Indian Ocean, this simple spritsail, two divergent spars holding up a tall rectangle of sail, may be the precursor of all spritsails. The name used is the earliest in English of which I am aware (Hornell, 1920*b*, p. 136). The sail also has been called "tall, rectangular spritsail" (Hornell, 1943, p. 41), "proto-Oceanic spritsail" (Bowen, 1953, p. 84), and "Indonesian spritsail" (Bowen, 1959, p. 156).

B. Common Spritsail (with or without boom). This sail is so commonly encountered in Western Europe that it is usually referred to in Western maritime literature simply as "spritsail" and rarely is particularized as "European spritsail" (Bowen, 1959, p. 156). Its occurrence also in China and scattered through Austronesia, sometimes without a boom, but more frequently with one, requires the name given here in order to distinguish it from three other types of Austronesian spritsail.

C,D,E. Oceanic Spritsail. The Oceanic

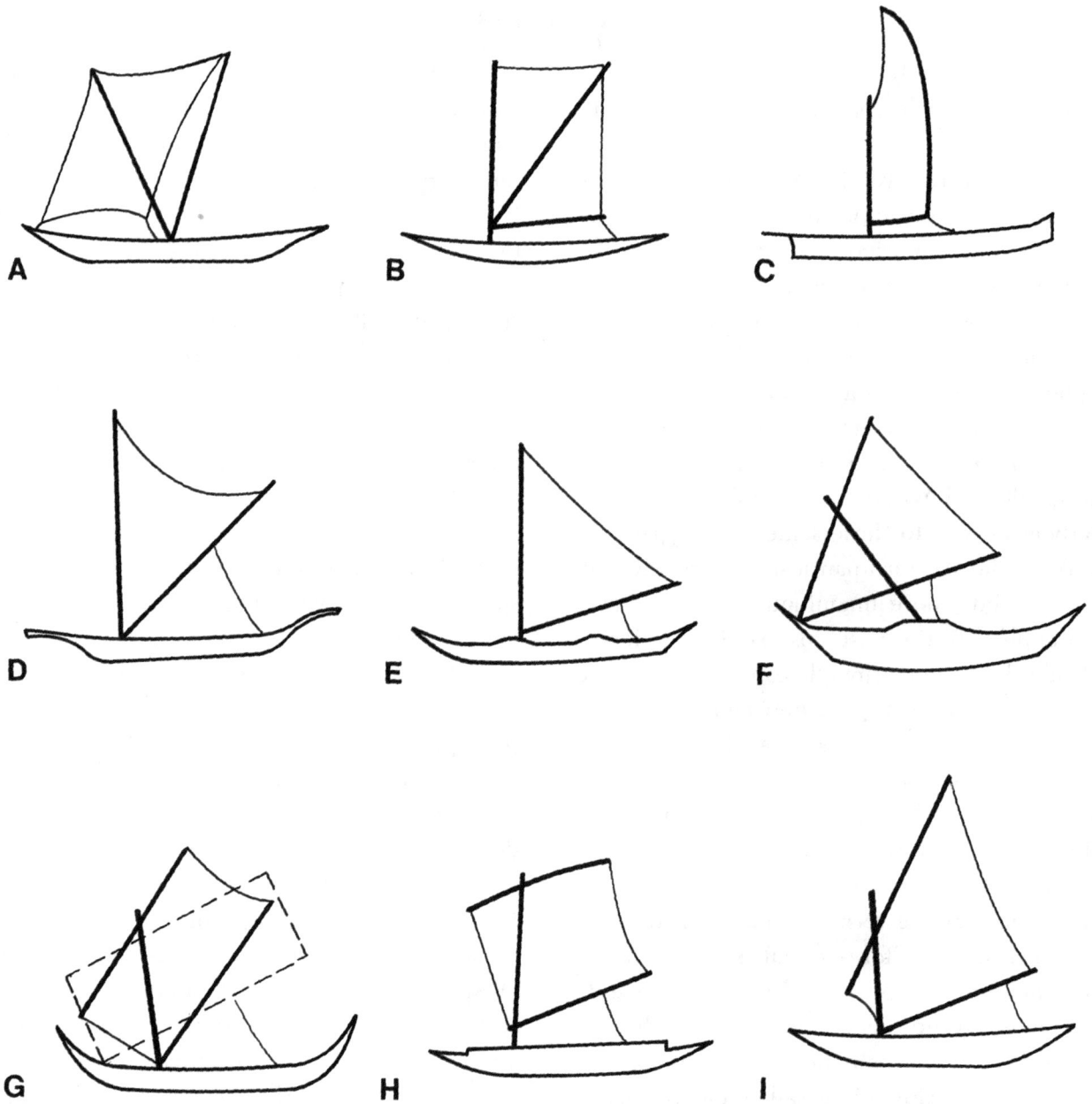

FIG. 21. Principal Austronesian sail types: *A*, double sprit, Sri Lanka; *B*, common sprit (boom), Philippines: *C*, Oceanic sprit, Tahiti; *D*, Oceanic sprit, Marquesas; *E*, Oceanic sprit, Sulu; *F*, crane sprit, Marshall Islands; *G*, rectangular boom lug, Moluccas; *H*, square boom lug, Gulf of Thailand; and *I*, trapezial boom lug, Vietnam.

sprit, so identified by Hornell (1936), is shown in three slightly different configurations. The most widespread and typical form by far is that shown in *D*. If the sprit gradually lowers toward the horizontal, at some point (by Western standards) it becomes a boom, a situation nearly reached in *E*. An even stranger arrangement of sprit is that shown in *C*. It has recently been suggested by David Lewis, whose opinion on nautical matters is not to be taken lightly and whose knowledge of Pacific navigation I consider definitive, that this sail should be called the "inverted, triangular sail" (1978, p. 56). I disagree on the basis that these sails meet the spritsail definition given above and also because of Hornell's precedence with a logical name. Lewis also suggests a category of "claw" sail for sails with a deeply incurved free edge and presents a reasoned case for functional efficiency of such sails (1978, p. 58). Again I feel forced to disagree, because the distribution of these sails (southeast Papuan coast, Reef Islands, and Hawaii) does not meet the requirement specified above that a type be conterminous. These sails seem to me to be simply an extreme form (perhaps, as Lewis points out, an extremely functional form) of the basic Oceanic spritsail.

F. Crane Spritsail. With this iconoclastic replacement for the conventional term *Oceanic lateen* I put myself in the unenviable position of disagreeing with every authority from Captain Cook to James Hornell—and most recently, David Lewis. (The logic of the argument which follows had better be good!)

In order to justify the assertion that this is a spritsail instead of a lateen (lugsail), we must refer to the nine sketches of Fig. 22. In all the sketches the points *A*, *B*, and *C* represent the head, clew, and tack of the sails and the lines *XY* represent the mast of the lateen rig and the pseudo-mast of the crane sprit. The drawings of the Mediterranean lateen indicate that it meets the definition of a lugsail: a sail hanging from a spar which is suspended in the air by the mast with more sail area aft than forward of the mast. A further implication is here made explicit; the yard of the lateen rotates on the mast at point *X* in order to adjust for different points of sailing. By contrast, the Oceanic spritsail has two divergent spars, but *AC* is the functional mast and is fixed in position. The sprit (nearly a boom) *BC* rotates from point *C* to adjust for different points of sailing. If we now look at the sketches of the crane sprit, we see that the basic design is the same as that shown in the sketches of the Oceanic sprit. The functional mast is spar *AC*, the sprit (or boom) *BC* swings out for adjustment, and spar *XY*, while sailing on a shunt, serves only to prop *AC* in position (aided by stays from *A* to the stern of the boat and to the center of the float). The other principal function of crane *XY* is exercised only during the shunting maneuver, when it carries the weight of the sail rig in shifting it from one end to the other (see Fig. 20*B*, stage 3). In other words, this sail is a specialized form of spritsail, and the superficial similarity with a lateen conceals a fundamental functional difference.

Deluded by this similarity, and having no vocabulary to describe the sail properly, Captain Cook (and all others since) called the shunting sail a lateen, an unfortunate choice in terminology which has caused confusion for two hundred years. Because both this sail and Mediterranean sails were "lateens," it often has been assumed that there must be some historical connection be-

Mediterranean Lateen

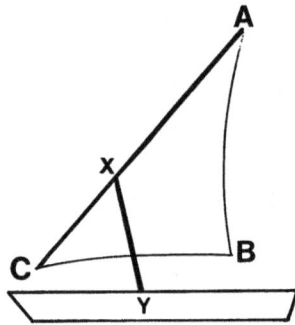

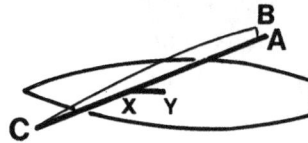

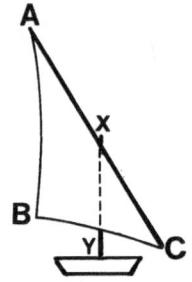

Oceanic Sprit

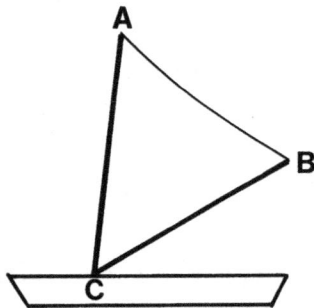

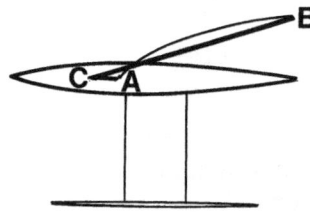

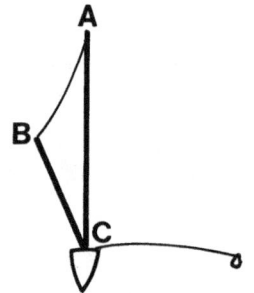

Crane Sprit (ex. Oceanic Lateen)

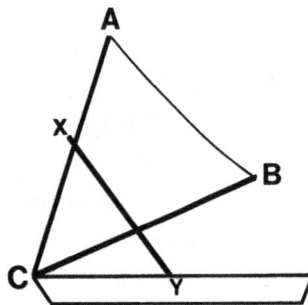

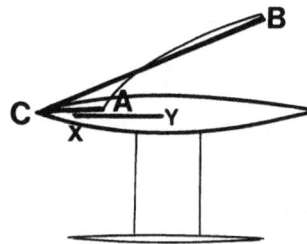

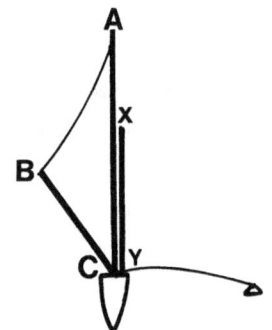

SIDE VIEW   TOP VIEW   FRONT VIEW

FIG. 22. Differences between lateen (lug) sails and spritsails.

FIG. 23. Primitive crane spritsail on a *tongiaki* double canoe of Tonga, late eighteenth century.

tween the two, despite the vast distance separating their two conterminous areas. If, on the other hand, we recognize that this sail is simply a specialized form of Oceanic sprit, devised to meet the technical needs of shunting, then all relationships fall comfortably into place in terms of Pacific culture history, and almost all sails of Polynesia, Micronesia, and Melanesia are genetically related spritsails.

In the early seventeenth century in Tonga, and later in Manihiki and the Tuamotus, some rather strange sails are recorded which clearly do not fall into the Oceanic sprit category because an extra spar is included in the rig. These we shall lump together, somewhat uncomfortably because of certain differences, into a category of "primitive crane spritsails." Hornell recognized them as "primitive lateen" sails (1936, p. 445). Data for Manihiki and the Tuamotus are too poor to allow satisfactory analysis, but an excellent series of drawings of Tongan double canoes made between 1616 and 1775 permits better understanding (Dodd, 1972, pp. 74–77). The latest and best drawing shows a vertical spar supported by three shrouds on each side which extend outward to a long cross-spar at deck level (Fig. 23). A short

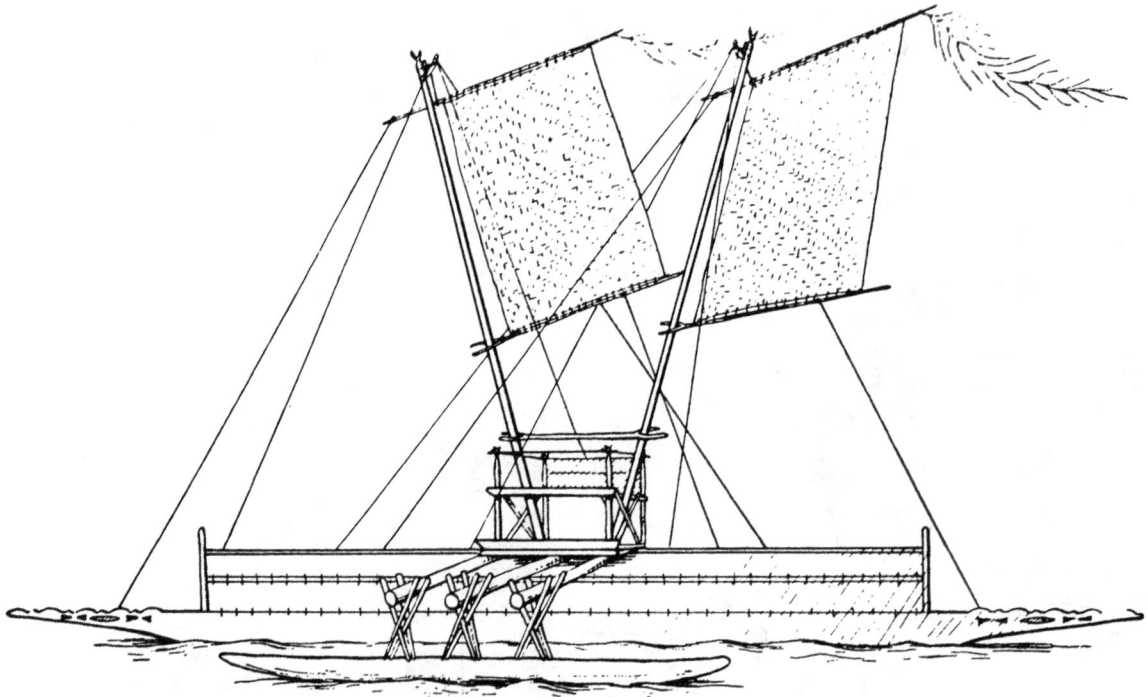

FIG. 24. Two-masted sailing canoe of Siassi, New Guinea.

forestay is visible, but the mast-sprit (to which the sail luff is attached) also is propped in place from behind by a spar which earlier observers thought was a mast. The lower sprit (nearly a boom) is attached to the foot of the sail. The rig cannot be classified as a lateen because the upper spar is stepped on deck and fixed in place by multiple shrouds. The supporting prop or crane must have been removed on each tack in order to permit the lower sprit (or boom) to swing across. When coupled with the advent of shunting in Manihiki and the Tuamotus, this curious sail appears to be a crude imitation of proper crane spritsails and part of the movement of the whole crane sprit and shunting technique toward the east.

G. Rectangular Boom Lugsail. First recog-

nized by Europeans as they moved into the East Indies in the early sixteenth century, this sail has caused more nomenclatural difficulty than any other in history. It would be burdensome to cite sources for all the names discovered thus far. Let me simply list those I have encountered: *lyre tanjong, sompot, leha, layag,* oblong mat, quadrangular, quadrilateral, rectangular lug, Indonesian lug, balance lug, Boro Bodur balance lug, dipping lug, standing lug, and canted square sail. The name suggested here as a standardized form comes first from the fact that the sail clearly meets the definition of a lugsail given above. To separate it from the two other great groups of lugs, those without booms and those with sail battens, the word *boom* must be used. And, finally, the rectangular shape differentiates the sail from two other types which are similar and closely related. The sail meets the two requirements for recognition as a type; general recognition and conterminous area.

A somewhat puzzling but seemingly related sail, which will be called the primitive rectangular lug, is found in western Melanesia (Fig. 24). The sail is made from a rectangular (occasionally oval) piece of matting, is bordered above and below by spars, and is suspended from and rotates around a mast, and hence meets the definition of a lugsail (except for having part before the mast). Although the sail is used on single-outrigger shunting canoes, unlike the rectangular boom lug which is used on double-outrigger tacking ca- noes, the sail is essentially contiguous with the Indonesian area and appears to be either a crude imitation of Indonesian sails or a primitive predecessor.

H, I. Square Boom Lugsail and Trapezial Boom Lugsail. These sails meet the same tests described above for the rectangular boom lug and are differentiated from it only on the basis of geo- metrical shape plus their own conterminous geo- graphical areas. The close relationship among the three types of boom lugs has long been noted (Nootebom, 1962, pp. 12–15; Poujade, 1946, p. 149), and in the proper place we shall look at the implications of that relationship toward culture history.

DESCRIPTIVE SUMMARY

In view of the mass of detail presented above about hulls, sailing techniques, and sail types, it is fortunate that there are canoe complexes among the various categories and separate distributions that make summarization relatively easy. In Poly- nesia both double canoes and single-outrigger canoes are found, almost always with Oceanic spritsails and using the technique of tacking. Mi- cronesia and Melanesia are for the most part char- acterized by single-outrigger canoes using crane spritsails to shunt from one side of the wind to the other. Double-outrigger canoes are found in In- donesia, always tacking and almost always using boom lugsails. In every case there are exceptions to the generalization which will be examined at appropriate points in the text and which will offer some of the most useful clues on canoe migrations and origins. At this point a broad-brush statement will serve as a useful first approximation for un- derstanding the topics which follow immediately.

3

Historical Sketch of Canoe Theories

〜〜〜〜〜〜〜〜〜〜〜〜〜〜〜〜〜〜〜〜〜〜〜〜〜〜〜〜〜〜

ALTHOUGH theories about canoe ages and origins are tied intimately to broader theories about the origins and migrations of Austronesian peoples, a review of the latter is beyond the scope of this book. Howard's essay "Polynesian Origins and Migrations" (1967) is an excellent "review of two centuries of speculation and theory" for those interested in the wider picture. We can, however, trace the thought of the two principal canoe authorities of the twentieth century, A. C. Haddon and James Hornell. Their substantive descriptions far exceed those of all other writers taken together, and their theoretical conclusions are still accepted by many students of Austronesian canoes.

Most writings about canoes by Haddon and Hornell were published in two decades which begin with a Haddon article (1918), continue with a series of papers separately by both authors, and culminate with the monumental *Canoes of Oceania*, on which they collaborated (1936–1938). Although their descriptive materials form the basis for all subsequent speculation about canoes, and indeed form the basis for this book, three constraints upon their theoretical reasoning

should be emphasized. They lived before radiocarbon dating made possible the construction of absolute chronologies, and they were forced to use only the type of time estimates made possible by the age-area theory and by guesses about the chronological meaning of islanders' genealogies. At the time they wrote, archaeology was essentially nonexistent in Austronesia, and such tools as relative chronology based on stratigraphy were denied them. Most significantly, they worked in a time dominated by wave theories of migration, the idea that the Pacific was periodically "inundated" by waves of migrants from some vague location in Southeast Asia bringing with them new sets of culture traits. In wave theory, one of the late migrations which reached far east into Polynesia was that of the "kava people," who brought with them fine, large double canoes and single-outrigger canoes. Small wonder, then, that they considered these craft younger than doubleoutrigger canoes despite evidence from their own work which was contradictory.

Although Haddon had worked in New Guinea and Queensland and had written on outriggers before the two decades of interest here, his work converged with Hornell's in a paper on East African outriggers in which he traced connections with Indonesia (1918). Hornell soon followed with a cluster of papers on the same topic (1919, 1920*a*, 1920*b*). It was in the 1920 papers that he set forth his hypothesis of relative ages, which was based on historical records in Madagascar which he interpreted as proving that single outriggers were replacing double outriggers and were therefore younger. As further evidence he presented a typological sequence showing the transition between the two.

The two historical bits are suggestive, not compelling, and the typology can be viewed as moving in the opposite direction to prove double outriggers to be younger. Hornell also neglects to mention that no single outriggers whatsoever are found along the African coast, where double outriggers are found from Lamu to Dar es Salaam. Taking the African evidence by itself, I do not see that it is conclusive in either direction on outrigger ages.

Next, the two authors shifted their examination to Indonesia, and two papers appeared almost simultaneously (Haddon, 1920; Hornell, 1920*c*). The descriptive material in these two papers, supplemented by Nooteboom's monograph (1932), was summarized in the Admiralty monograph of World War II (Great Britain, Admiralty, 1944*b*) and constitutes most of our knowledge of Indonesian craft. (Three short but useful monographs by Horridge [1978, 1979*a*, and 1979*b*] recently have contributed new insights on changes of the last five hundred years in canoe construction techniques in Sulawesi and the Moluccas.)

Haddon's and Hornell's theoretical conclusions on canoe ages are fascinating because they came to diametrically opposed views based on exactly the same evidence. To Haddon the double outrigger was "early" because it could be dated to A.D. 800 by the Boro Bodur sculptures; was peripheral (hence early) because of relict examples in Palau, the Marquesas, and Easter Island; and was less seaworthy, hence likely to be replaced by the single outrigger (1920, pp. 100, 122). Hornell, however, considered the distribution of the double outrigger in Indonesia to be central (hence later) and the seaworthiness of the double outrigger to be superior to that of the single outrigger (1920*c*, pp. 104–106). A little later Hornell repeated his distributional argument (1923, p. 228), and still later, in the first volume of *Canoes of Oceania*, he proved that double outriggers had *not* existed as relics in the peripheral locations claimed by Haddon (1936, pp. 31, 100, 437).

Perhaps due to differences of opinion and acknowledgedly due to the complexity of Oceanic prehistory, the two authors in their summary volume of *Canoes of Oceania* are so cautious that they are almost disappointing. They discuss several theories on the origin of outriggers but make no selection among them (Haddon and Hornell, 1938, p. 19), and they later present ten theories on the possible origins of double canoes, single outriggers, and double outriggers, again without making any decisions among them (pp. 41–44). In their judgment, sail types, in order from oldest to youngest, are the Oceanic sprit, Oceanic lateen, and quadrangular sails (p. 55). Strangely, in view of the emphasis in 1920, no mention is made of the controversial topic of seaworthiness. Finally, the wave theory of migration eastward is advocated, the earliest wave a group of people who were proto-Melanesian in stock and culture and

Austronesian in speech and who used double-outrigger canoes with square sails. The second wave used double canoes and single outriggers rigged with Oceanic spritsails. Still later arrived kava people in double canoes, and finally came betel people who brought the *mon* outriggerless canoe of the Solomon Islands (pp. 76–79). Only at this point are relative canoe ages finally advocated, and the contradiction with sail ages (p. 55) is not noted. Age-area arguments are abandoned presumably because the wave theory contradicts them.

Hornell's final word on the matter, his book *Water Transport* (1946), is brief and to the point. Double outriggers developed in mainland Southeast Asia or nearby island Indonesia from sponsons or balance platforms on both sides of canoes which aided stability and provided poling platforms (p. 268). Single outriggers developed farther out in the island world of larger waves and more dangerous voyages because of their greater seaworthiness (p. 269). Finally, double canoes were developed from single outriggers in Polynesia for greater carrying capacity (p. 263). The central distribution of double-outrigger canoes and inferences from the age-area hypothesis are not mentioned. In twenty-five years, Hornell's contradictory views on Madagascar and Indonesia (1920*b* and 1920*c*) have been resolved and he has come to a position which approximates Haddon's. For nearly thirty years no one questioned Hornell's statements in *Water Transport*, and his position is probably the conventional wisdom of today. Some years ago (1974) I presented in a short paper a series of arguments tending to indicate that double-outrigger canoes were more youthful than double canoes and single outriggers. This book presents the opportunity to bring the linguistic and archaeological aspects of the problem up to date and to elaborate on the technological and distributional analyses which could only be sketched in the short paper.

4

The Anthropological Evidence for
Cultural Movements

By the Second World War, two centuries of study and speculation by a wide assortment of explorers, missionaries, and scientists had produced a picture of the Austronesian area which still holds generally today (cf. Howard, 1967; also see Fig. 1). To the east lies Polynesia, distinguished by a hierarchical and largely patrilineal social system and by people of proto-Mongoloid descent. To the west, and north of the equator, is Micronesia, not much different from Polynesia except in such esoterica as a strong tendency toward matrilineal descent and some evidence of race mixing with people to the south. Melanesia is easily distinguishable by Australoid race, black to dark brown skin and frizzy hair, and a capitalist tendency toward social climbing by means of entrepreneurship and feast-giving; languages are a complex mix of Austronesian and Papuan tongues. Indonesia, farther west, is related to the first two culture areas in proto-Mongoloid race and Austronesian languages, but it is much more advanced, with iron tools and seed agriculture superimposed on the basic Oceanic horticulture. Madagascar, far to the west, is clearly a relatively recent offshoot from Indonesia.

The last three decades have brought significant advances in our understanding of Oceanic culture history. The best modern opinion in physical anthropology (see Howells, 1977, and 1973 for a book-length statement) is that probably only two races exist in Oceania, proto-Mongoloids and Australoids (see Fig. 25). From Indochina to Easter Island (except in Melanesia) race is much the same, although disguised by relatively small differences resulting from the genetic drift implicit in small founder populations. Differences can be detected between Melanesians and Australian aborigines, but again they basically belong together racially. More characteristic Mongoloids, epicanthic fold and all, are found in China and northward. The Mongoloid–African Negroid mixture which characterizes Madagascar is a much more recent and completely different matter than the Mongoloid–Australoid clines found at the eastern and western extremities of Melanesia. (Indian "Caucasoids" are included on the map in cavalier disregard of arguments about Negroids and Veddoids simply to indicate that what are probably relatively recent outrigger distributions in Ceylon and on the Indian coasts do not have racial implications for the main problems herein discussed.)

Radiocarbon dates of 30,000 B.C. and earlier in Australia and almost as early in New Guinea

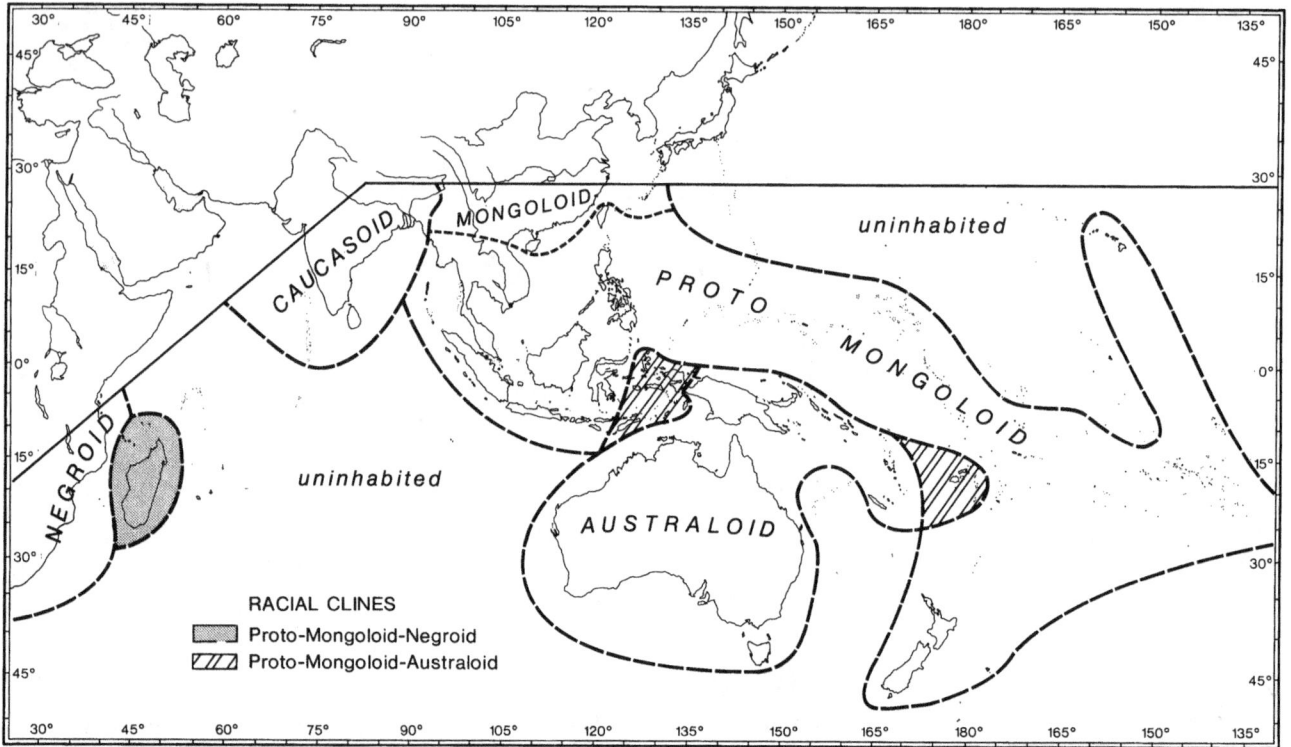

FIG. 25. Racial distributions.

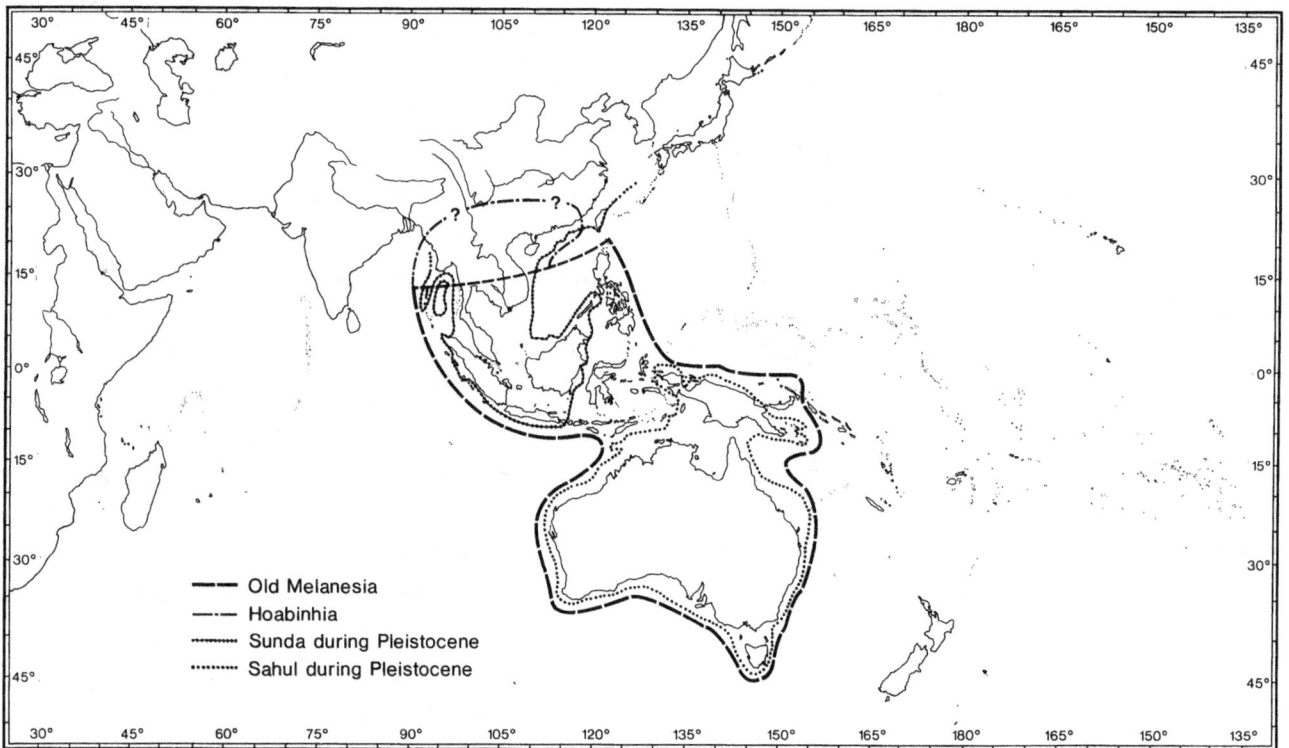

FIG. 26. Old Melanesia and Hoabinhia.

demonstrate an ancient eastward movement of Australoid peoples, very likely during lowered sea levels of the Pleistocene, into New Guinea, the Bismarcks, Australia, and Tasmania (Fig. 26). Between the land of the exposed Sunda Shelf (now flooded to produce island Indonesia) and the similarly exposed Sahul Shelf (now separated into the four areas just mentioned) lie deep channels which were water barriers of forty miles or more even when sea levels were 450 feet lower than they are at present. Men crossed these barriers, perhaps on very simple log rafts or bark boats, to occupy the southeastern portion of "Old Melanesia" and thus provide the earliest firm evidence presently known for water transport (see Birdsell, 1977, for an extensive examination of this problem). Movements farther eastward of men, for the most part of proto-Mongoloid race, did not occur for several tens of thousands of years until canoe technology was far more advanced.

Major post–World War II developments have taken place in linguistics and archaeology. An admirable archaeological summary, including physical landscape, race, and ethnology, is provided by Bellwood in a terse but inclusive paper on the prehistory of Oceania (1975). More heavily weighted toward linguistics but including the most recent archaeological evidence and a summary is a paper by Shutler and Marck which is concerned with the dispersal of Austronesian horticulturists (1975). An extended monograph on Oceanic prehistory by Shutler and Shutler (1975), a book-length expansion of his brief paper by Bellwood (1979), and a prehistory of Polynesia edited by Jennings (1979) provide far more detail. The comments which follow, primarily oriented

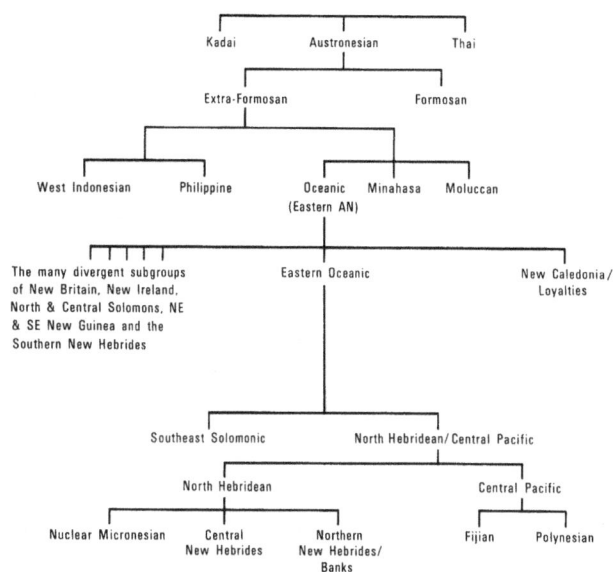

FIG. 27. Austronesian linguistic relationships.

toward watercraft, are taken from these sources.

A great deal of rigorous analysis of languages has produced understanding of the genetic relationships expressed in Fig. 27. It is now evident that Polynesian language and culture developed in the Fiji-Tonga-Samoa area about 1000 B.C. and thence spread eastward. Relationships to languages far to the west are distant, and wave theories of repeated migration are clearly outdated. Watercraft, as much as other culture traits which now are found in Polynesia, developed from those already in existence in Fiji-Samoa, hence a late wave of double canoes and single outriggers from island southeast Asia is out of the question.

The most exciting development from extensive archaeological investigations of recent decades is recognition of a pottery type, Lapita, which extends from eastern New Guinea to Tonga and Samoa and is largely restricted in time to the first millennium B.C. (Fig. 28). At the eastern end, Lapitalike pottery extends as far as the Marquesas in the early centuries of the Christian era. Since only proto-Mongoloid peoples of Polynesian culture (including double canoes and single-outrigger canoes) are found to the east, there is an inclination, unsupported by firm evidence, to consider that these eastern relationships with Lapita also are true as far west as the Bismarck Archipelago. Obsidian from the Talasea Peninsula of New Britain has been found as far east as the Santa Cruz Islands and New Caledonia, and it is exciting to hypothesize a pre-Polynesian group of Austronesian speakers trading back and forth for a millennium, using double canoes as transport. A summary map showing routes and times of the Austronesian horticulturist dispersion, based primarily on linguistic data but agreeing broadly with archaeological evidence, is presented in Fig. 29 (Shutler and Marck, 1975).

Covariation among race, language, and other aspects of culture is nicely apparent in Polynesia and Indonesia; proto-Mongoloids speaking Austronesian tongues go about their horticultural business in more or less hierarchical societies. Australia also is pleasantly consistent: Australoids speaking probably Papuan-related tongues hunt and collect their food. Patterns fall apart a bit in Micronesia, with some evidence of race mixing and dominance of matrilineal groupings. But the whole pattern of covariation disintegrates in Melanesia. Language may be Papuan or Austronesian; race is dominantly Australoid, but with evidence of mixing and with largely Mongoloid populations in the "Polynesian outliers" nearby; both patrilineal and matrilineal descent is followed; nonhierarchical societies dominate, with feast-giving as the route to social success; and yet a uniform horticultural way of life is followed. The explicit contradictions are bewildering, and no generally accepted culture history which explains them is at hand. Bypassing Melanesia through Micronesia to allow Polynesians to reach their culture area unmixed with Australoid race and Papuan speech was a common hypothesis forty years ago (Buck, 1938) and has been reopened as a hypothesis, largely on a basis of race (Howells, 1973). More generally accepted are two versions which get Polynesian ancestors through Melanesia, either preceding the movement of Melanesians into the Solomons, New Hebrides, New Caledonia, and Fiji or as an endogamous coastal and seafaring group which bypassed Melanesians living mostly in the interiors of large islands. Neither hypothesis seems dominant at present. Let us now turn, in the next two chapters, to evidence specifically related to boats and their history and inferentially of assistance in understanding Austronesian culture history as a whole.

5

Seaworthiness of Austronesian Canoes

~~~~~~

WE have already seen that estimates of seaworthiness of different canoe configurations have played a role in hypotheses about their relative ages. In order to bolster their ideas, writers have blithely broken off floats of double outriggers by wave action to form single outriggers, capsized almost every configuration more readily than any other, and asserted rank orders of seaworthiness based on no evidence whatsoever. It is particularly writers such as Haddon, who provides excellent static descriptions but almost no information on how boats perform at sea, who have made dataless allegations. Even James Hornell, who knew more about primitive craft than anyone else and had considerable knowledge of seamanship, changed his mind completely between 1920 and 1946 as to the seaworthiness of double-outrigger canoes—and with nothing more than assertions to justify the turnabout. In my earlier brief article (1974), for lack of space and of sufficient analysis at the time, I also made some assertions about seaworthiness which were mostly allegations supported by a few bits of evidence. A more rigorous study of the matter, based on the facts of canoe construction and performance as we can reconstruct them and employing modern understanding of the physics of sailing craft, seems overdue.

The examination of relative seaworthiness of canoes which follows provides strong support for the argument that Polynesian double canoes and single outriggers which are tacked head to wind are seaworthy and are the oldest types. The evidence also indicates that single outriggers (and the rare double canoes) of Micronesia and Melanesia which are shunted from tack to tack are even more seaworthy and are intermediate in age. Finally, the analysis suggests that Indonesian double-outrigger canoes, which are tacked head to wind, are the most seaworthy and youngest of Austronesian canoe types.

SIMILARITIES IN SEAWORTHINESS

In an effort to reduce the ambiguity of the term *seaworthiness*, a baker's dozen of somewhat arbitrary components, all contributing to this characteristic, will be isolated and examined individually. Eight of the thirteen seaworthiness components recognized here are much the same for all types of Oceanic canoes, and seven of them, well known to students of Pacific canoes, need to

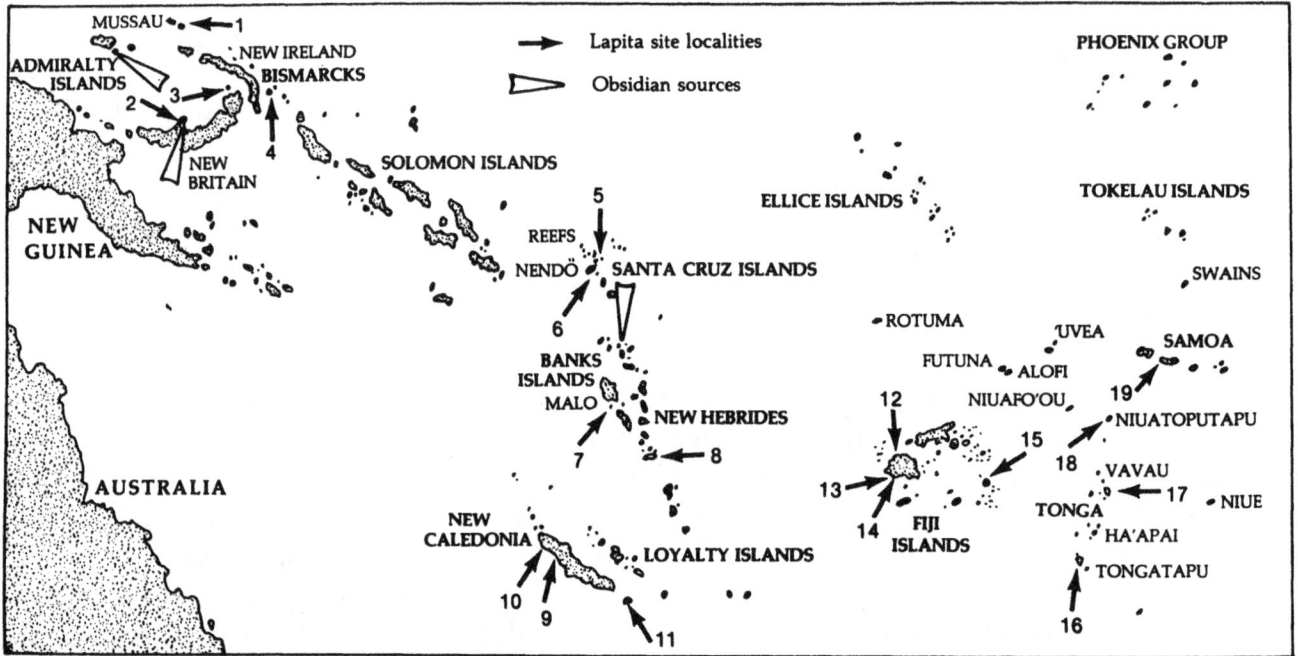

FIG. 28. Distribution of Lapita pottery sites.

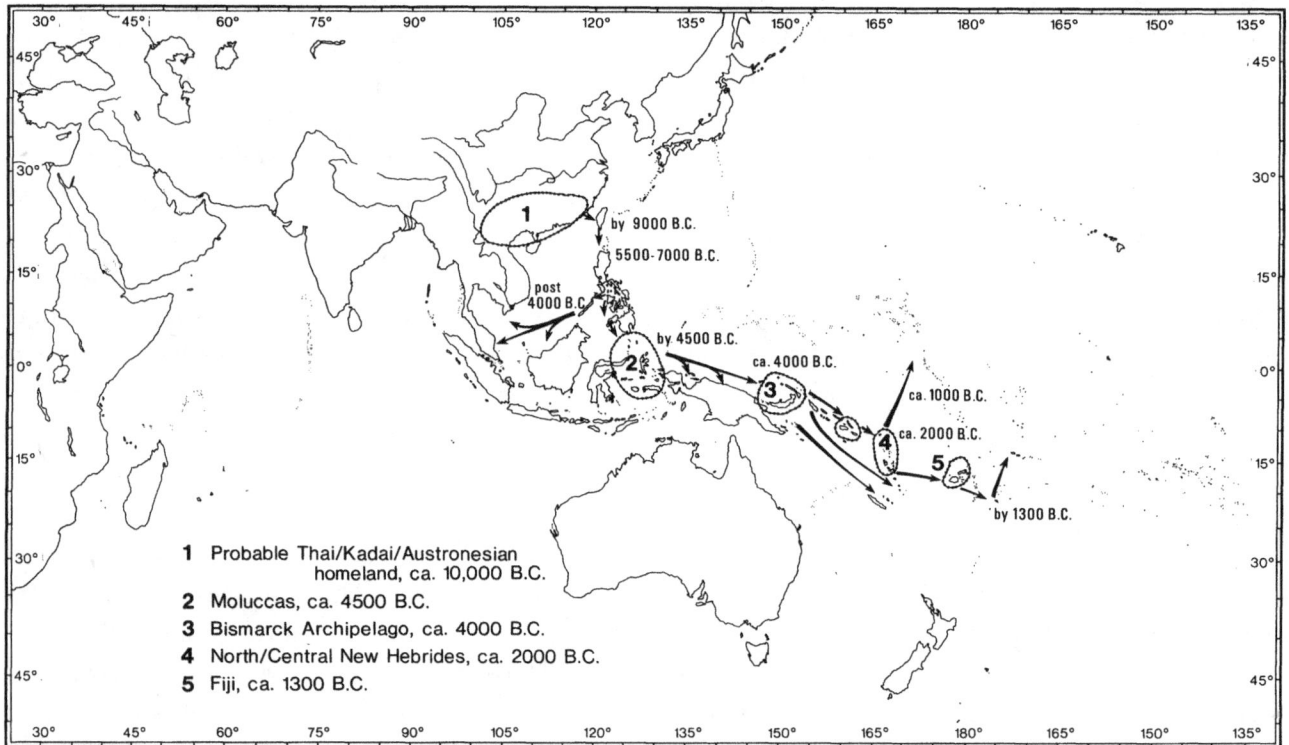

1 Probable Thai/Kadai/Austronesian
       homeland, ca. 10,000 B.C.
2 Moluccas, ca. 4500 B.C.
3 Bismarck Archipelago, ca. 4000 B.C.
4 North/Central New Hebrides, ca. 2000 B.C.
5 Fiji, ca. 1300 B.C.

FIG. 29. Primary Austronesian dispersals in the Pacific.

be discussed only briefly. The eighth component, stability, will be examined in more detail.

1. *Size*. Over the breadth of the Pacific, canoes vary in size from small, ten-foot paddling canoes to vessels which really might be called small ships. Canoes over one hundred feet in length are recorded from Hawaii, the Tuamotus, Tahiti, Fiji (Hornell, 1936, pp. 19, 80, 135, 307), the Gilberts (Lewis, 1972, p. 263), and Sulu (Doran, forthcoming). Canoes in the range of fifty to seventy-five feet in length are common everywhere, and there is no good correlation between size and canoe type, although the largest boats in Polynesia usually were double canoes. Size alone is not enough to guarantee seaworthiness, as we can see by comparing *Mikael* (Figs. 10–12), a seaworthy boat about twenty-five feet long, with *Nalehia* (Fig. 7), which is much less seaworthy at a length of forty-two feet. Nevertheless, all types of Pacific canoes are constructed in sizes (plus other considerations) which make them reasonably seaworthy.

2. *Materials and Structure*. All Pacific canoes are constructed of wood, and most are built in the same way. A basal log is hollowed into a dugout upon which one or more side planks or strakes are lashed to increase the freeboard. In a few places (the Tuamotus, Solomons, and Moluccas, for example) the basal log is much reduced in size, planking sometimes is almost a patchwork, and frames are inserted to insure adequate strength. Because of this fundamental similarity in type and strength of materials, no differentiation as to seaworthiness is possible.

3. *Decks and Freeboard*. No Austronesian canoes have watertight decks. In a few places poor substitutes are found in the form of mat covers with manholes for paddlers (for example, *Nalehia*, Fig. 7) or partly decked bows and sterns. On the other hand, voyaging canoes frequently have freeboards greater than two and one-half feet and are relatively safe in most sea states (cf. *Mikael*, Fig. 12, and *Hokule'a*, Fig. 6). In sum, large canoes with adequate freeboard are found in all parts of the Pacific, and no differentiation among them is possible on this basis. All are reasonably seaworthy.

4. *Hull Form*. Implicit in the built-up canoe design, strakes added to a basal dugout, is the long and narrow form which characterizes all Pacific canoes. Length-to-beam ratios range from a low of about 9 to a maximum of 20 or more, and beam-to-depth ratios may be as small as 0.5. Western and Chinese craft, by comparison, typically have length-to-beam ratios of about 3 and beam-to-depth ratios of about 2, an empirically derived set of dimensions which provides enough stability to carry sail and yet a width which does not create excessive water resistance or drag. Boats of the Pacific canoe shape are unseaworthy even as paddling canoes and can carry only tiny sails without capsizing. But with the addition of stabilizing devices such as outriggers, they can be converted into seaworthy craft.

5. *Light Displacement*. Long and narrow boats cannot carry much cargo but have the compensating potential for speed because of their light weight as well as shape. No ballast was used in the Pacific, and nearly all cargoes, including men, had specific gravities of about one or well below; hence, Oceanic canoes were unsinkable. They could swamp or break up, but they remained afloat. In this respect all canoes were equally seaworthy.

6. *Speed*. Long, narrow, and light boats have considerable speed potential, and all Austronesian canoes were alike in this respect. Narrow boats penetrate the water with less opposition (have lower "form resistance") than do broad ones, but if they are excessive in length, they have so much wetted surface area that friction with the water ("skin friction") tends to slow them. In achieving the least resistance toward movement ("minimum drag"), the tradeoff point between form resistance and skin friction lies somewhere between length-to-beam ratios of 10 and 20. Modern authorities differ on this point (Norwood asserts that 12 to 16 is optimal; 1979, p. 17), but all Oceanic canoes were in the proper range of design to achieve fast speeds compared to European craft of the day. Up to a point, speed may be considered an attribute of seaworthiness, whether as a factor in reducing the time for an interisland voyage or in reaching a safe harbor or beach before a storm breaks.

7. *Righting Ability*. All Austronesian canoes, whatever their stabilizing system, could be capsized, and once upside down they were just as stable as in upright position. Nothing is known about righting techniques used on large vessels (over thirty or forty feet), but the technical problem was immense. Righting of smaller canoes, twenty-five to thirty feet long, particularly those with single outriggers, presents less of a problem, and techniques for so doing are known for Micronesia and Tahiti (Doran, 1972, p. 158; Hornell, 1936, p. 121). By standing on the float or by rigging a small tripod on the capsized boat and outrigger, enough crew weight can be exerted to force the float down and under the hull, whereupon it rises by its own buoyancy on the other side, righting the canoe. In the absence of information on most types of canoes, especially larger ones, all we can say is that the problem was ubiquitous, but no ranking among canoe types can be ascertained.

8. *Stability*. All of the long, narrow, unstable canoes of the Pacific were converted to seaworthy, stable craft by means of balancing appendages thrust out to one or both sides. The three different techniques used were, of course, the double equal or subequal hulls in the double canoe, the single float extended on one side of the single-outrigger canoe, and the two floats, one on either side, of the double-outrigger canoe. In every case the stability required to carry sail came from a righting force equal to the weight and/or buoyancy of a hull or float(s) multiplied by the lever arm from float(s) (or hull) to point of rotation (see Fig. 30). Crew weights could be adjusted in or out to increase stability and were increasingly important in smaller craft. It is important to note that in Figs. 30C and D the total float buoyancy is much less than the total boat weight, hence a capsize involves rotation about the hull, not the float.

Wind capsizing force is a function of sail area times the lever arm (height to the center of effort of the sail) times wind speed squared times a factor of 0.003394 (one-half the mass density of air and in units that allow use of wind speed in knots; see Marchaj, 1964 and 1979, p. 168, for details). Capsizing force of the sail rig is a simple function of the weight of the rig times the height to the center of weight. As the boat heels at an increasing angle, the hull righting force diminishes (with the cosine of the heel angle), the sail rig capsizing force increases (with the sine of the angle), and

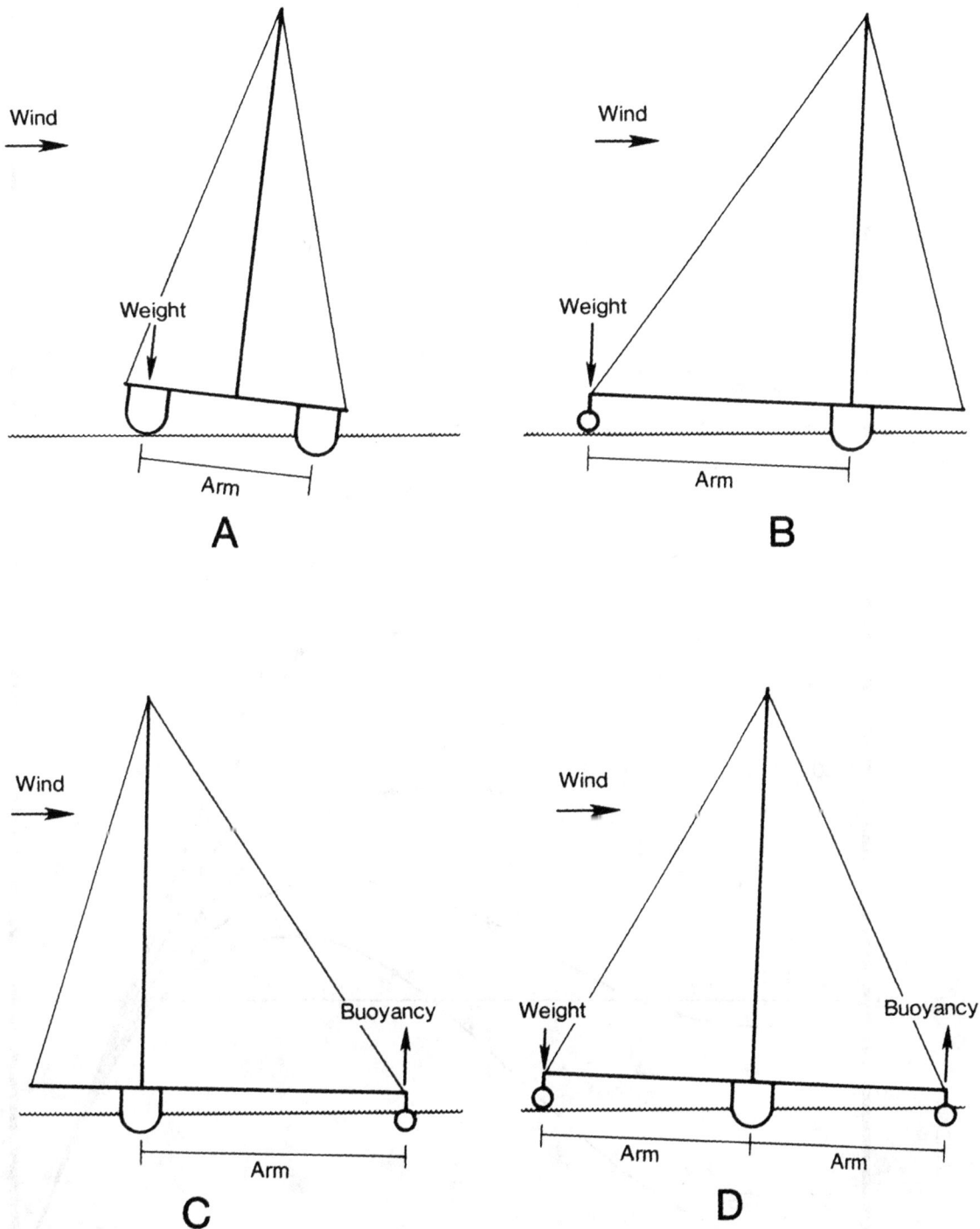

FIG. 30. Maximum stability in four configurations: A, double canoe with weather hull just clear of water; B, single-outrigger canoe with float to weather just clear of water; C, single-outrigger canoe with float to leeward and just submerged; D, double-outrigger canoe with weather float clear of water and lee float just submerged.

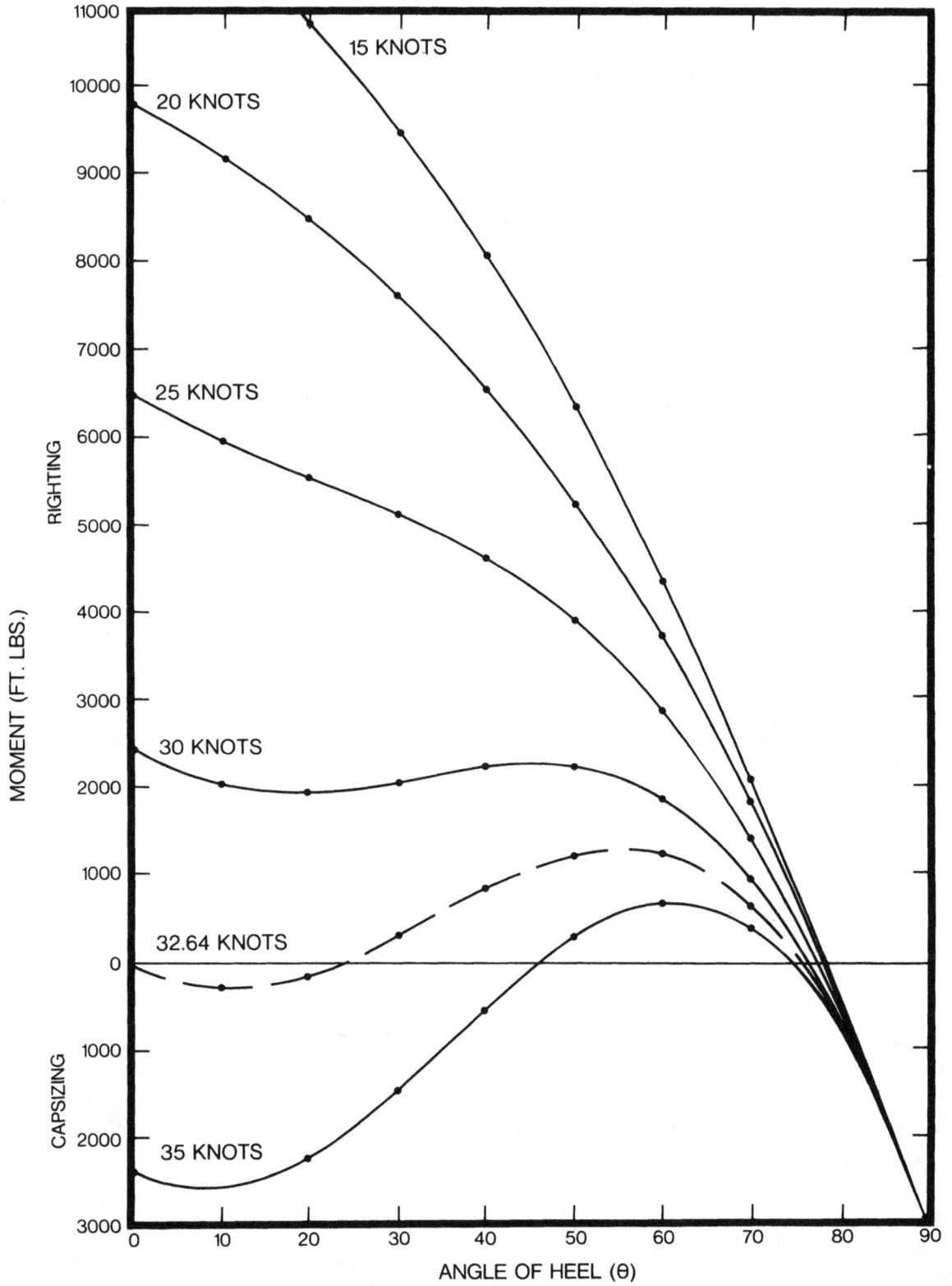

FIG. 31. Stability curves for double canoe *Nalehia*.

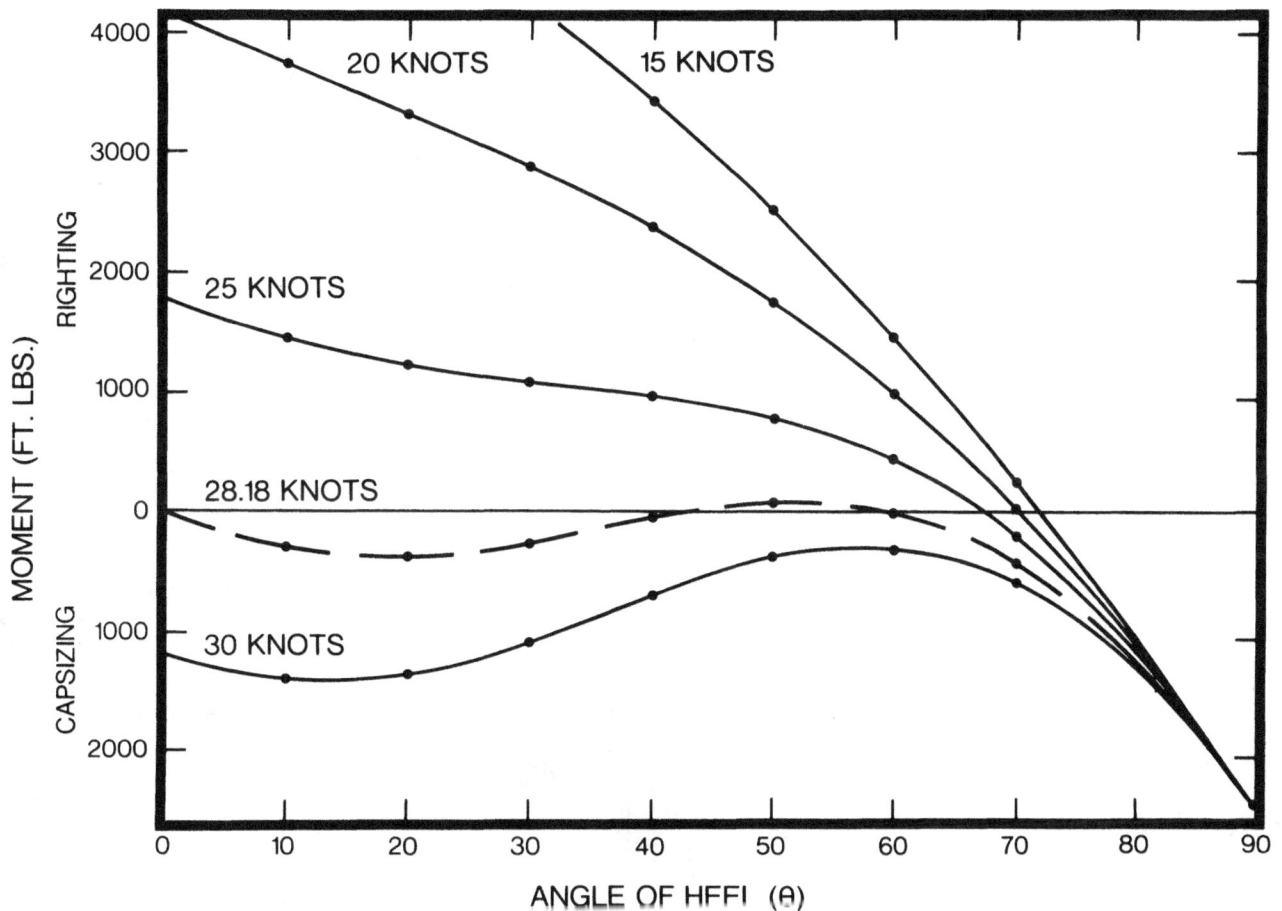

FIG. 32. Stability curves for single-outrigger canoe *Mikael*.

the wind force on the sail decreases (with the cosine squared of the angle) (Norwood, 1976, p. 6). An equation which adds these forces algebraically gives a result in foot-pounds of force which may be positive (a net righting moment) or negative (a net capsizing moment).*

*This first approximation of the forces operating on a sailing vessel has been improved by Stover's much more sophisticated (but difficult and time-consuming) analysis (1978). In the absence of any data on lift and drag ratios for Oceanic sails, and because the more rapid first approximation is reasonably accurate, it is used here (also see Doran, 1979).

With this equation, stability curves have been calculated for three types of Oceanic canoes, based on the field data of Table 1, and are shown in Figs. 31–33. Stability moment is plotted against heel angle for several wind speeds. Note that the basic shapes of the curves for double canoes, single outriggers, and double outriggers are similar (as are those for modern catamarans, proas, and trimarans). As wind forces increase, the curves progressively flatten and then reverse into S-shapes. This reversal takes place because

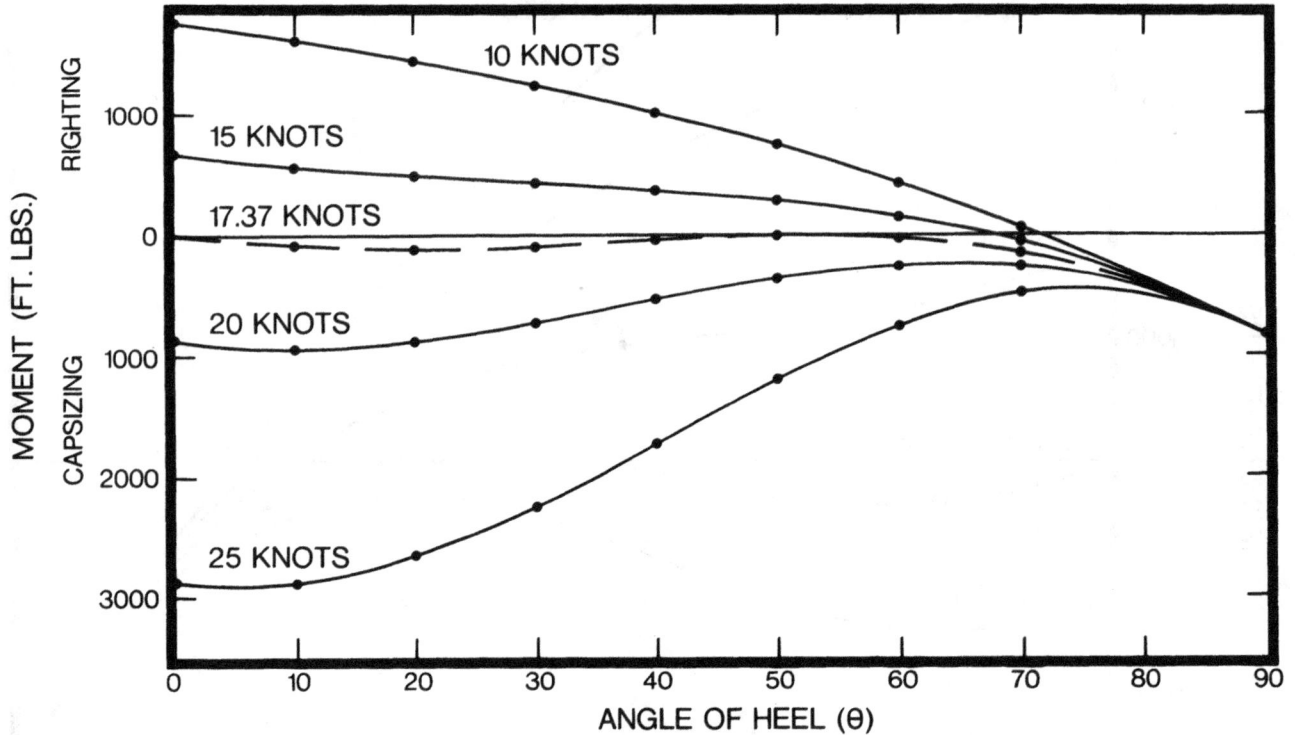

FIG. 33. Stability curves for double-outrigger canoe *Nardi*.

the wind force decreases with the cosine squared of the heel angle while stability decreases only with the cosine of the angle. The wind force, which has increased (on successive curves) with the square of the wind speed, thus decreases very quickly with increasing heel angle. For example, as shown in Fig. 31, the windward hull of the double canoe *Nalehia* will lift clear of the water at a wind speed of just under 33 knots, and the canoe will heel over to about 25° and will stabilize at that point because righting and capsizing forces are precisely balanced. If the wind speed drops a bit, the hull also will drop back into the water. But if the wind speed increases to 35 knots, the canoe will heel to about 45° and again stabilize because

the upward-trending stability curve has again reached the balance point between righting and capsizing forces. It is obvious that the conventional view, that instantaneous capsize results once a hull leaves the water, is incorrect.

The S-shape of stability curves for multi-hulled craft of all types permits the modern catamaran sailor to "fly a hull" for considerable distances and also was the factor that made it possible for a young Micronesian to "fly the float" of his single-outrigger canoe for the prescribed distance that proved him to be a competent sailor. This enormously valuable safety factor in sailing such craft in any sector from close-hauled to a beam reach or beyond must have saved many lives in the past. It may be no great exaggeration to suggest that the settlement of the Pacific was in considerable measure made possible by the increase in seaworthiness inherent in this family of stability curves.

Although this safety factor applies on the most dangerous points of sailing, close-hauled to beam reach, it should be emphasized that it declines in significance as wind-heeling forces decline on a broad reach to a run. If by some unusual mischance on such a course a windward hull (of a double canoe) or float (of a single outrigger) rises clear of the water, the boat will capsize almost instantly. The hull righting force (decreasing with the cosine of the heel angle) and sail rig capsizing force (increasing with the sine of the heel angle) combine to produce a curve which is convex upward and hence a total capsizing force which accelerates with heel angle. (I learned this lesson the hard way by sailing a small proa downwind and attempting to reduce drag by hiking out and lifting the float out of water. The capsize which followed was practically instantaneous.)

The eight components of seaworthiness thus far examined have been essentially equal for the three major configurations of canoes in the Pacific. It should be emphasized again that all canoe types are seaworthy, that all permitted long voyages across the ocean, and that the form of their stability curves in particular means that multi-hulled craft are forgiving of mistakes in handling. There are distinctions, however, among the several configurations.

DIFFERENCES IN SEAWORTHINESS

Although several kinds of differences can be recognized among double canoes, single outriggers, and double outriggers, no good method of quantifying them appears to be available. For each of the following components I shall simply order the canoes by rank, assigning three points to a "good" canoe, two points to a "better" type, and one point to the "best" type. In cases which seem about equal, the sum of the two rank orders will be halved and applied to each.

1. *Hull Construction Technique*. With minor variations, a single hull construction technique is used throughout Polynesia, Micronesia, and Melanesia (Hornell, 1936; Haddon, 1937; and Haddon and Hornell, 1938, *passim*). When strakes are added to the basic dugout, their edges may be chamfered a bit, but in many cases the plank edges are simply sided together, then held in place by firm lashings through holes pecked into the planks. Slices of green, compressible coconut husk, with sticky breadfruit gum as adhesive and water repellent, are placed between the plank edges in Micronesia, and modifications of this basic technique are used elsewhere. If greater length is required, planks usually are butt-joined without any scarfs, although crude scarfs are known in the Marquesas and New Zealand (Hornell, 1936, pp. 46, 97). In Indonesia, however, techniques are more sophisticated and result in stronger hulls. Holes are bored in opposing plank edges, dowels are inserted, and the new strake is forced down on the dowels into a tight joint which will not permit lateral movement of one plank edge relative to the next (Collins, 1937,

pp. 9–109; Hornell, 1920*c*, p. 59; Horridge, 1978, p. 27; Wallace, 1869, p. 425). If scarfs are required, they are made diagonally, with an overlap equal to plank width. No great differences are found farther east, but the Indonesian construction technique is clearly stronger. Ranking: double outrigger, 1; single outrigger and double canoe, 2.5 each.

2. *Stability and Speed.* At a given wind speed, the maximum speed at which a boat can sail is a function of the maximum sail area it can carry without capsizing divided by the boat's weight. Under racing conditions (near shore with rescuers at hand and low expected wind speeds) both modern and primitive craft have carried incredible amounts of sail, but in comparing Pacific canoes, we shall assume voyaging conditions across the high seas and then try to ascertain differences, if any, among the several configurations.

2A. Speed from historical sources. The large voyaging double canoes and single outriggers of Polynesia were replaced by European craft more than a century ago; thus, our knowledge of their sailing speed depends on vague historical references (Hornell, 1936, pp. 18, 20, 25, 84, 121, 124, 127, 232, 239, 241). Comments range from "a dull sailer" to "go at a very good rate." On average they indicate reasonably good sailing performance but nothing particularly startling to early observers. By contrast, the shunting double canoes of Fiji and single outriggers throughout Micronesia were considered unusually fast by all observers. A Fijian double canoe made twelve knots, Gilbertese boats were called "flying proas" (seventeen knots recorded), and a Carolines canoe averaged fourteen knots on a

trip from Guam to Manila (Hornell, 1936, pp. 327, 350, 417). Farther west, in Indonesia, the written evidence again is inexact, but the comments available indicate relatively high speeds for double-outrigger canoes. Minahasa canoes (North Sulawesi) showed high speed under sail (Hornell, 1920*c*, p. 86), and other boats had "high" and "marvelous" speeds (Haddon, 1920, pp. 93, 106). On the basis of limited evidence, it probably is fair to rank Polynesian craft as 3 and to give a shared ranking of 1.5 to Micronesian and Indonesian boats.

2B. Estimated speeds of three existing canoes. To my knowledge, only five canoes in the Pacific have had both lines and performance measured with modern instruments: two modern double canoe analogues in Hawaii (*Hokule'a* and *Nalehia*), two shunting single-outrigger canoes of Puluwat Atoll in Micronesia (*Mikael* and *Epifano*), and one double-outrigger canoe in Sulu (*Nardi*) (Doran, 1972, 1975; Finney, 1977). The boats measured include all three of the basic canoe types, but no data exist for tacking single outriggers.

A good estimate of sailing speed comes from the Bruce number (Br), which is the square root of sail area divided by the cube root of the total weight, including crew and gear, while sailing. Bruce numbers can be calculated for these well-documented boats (see Bruce and Morss, 1976, pp. 97–98, for a discussion of this number), and as listed in Table 1, *Nalehia*, the Hawaiian double canoe, has Br = 0.84; *Mikael*, the Micronesian single outrigger, has Br = 1.04; and *Nardi*, the Sulu double outrigger, has Br = 1.33. By comparison, the square-rigger *Flying Cloud* had Br = 0.88; a modern offshore racing yacht, *On-*

TABLE 1. Data for Canoes of Three Types.

Dimensions and Calculated Data	Double Canoe *Nalehia* (Fig. 7)	Single-Outrigger *Mikael* (Figs. 10–12)	Double-Outrigger *Nardi* (Figs. 15–17)
Length overall (ft.)	42.2	25.8	24.5
Hull beam (ft.)	2.0	2.1	1.7
Beam overall (ft.)	7.5	13.7	13.5
Sail area, A_s (sq. ft.)	210	220	237
Weight with crew (lb.)	5,060	2,900	1,600
Bruce number ($\sqrt{A_s} \div \sqrt[3]{\text{Wt.}}$)	0.84	1.04	1.33
Height to center of effort, *CE*, of sail (ft.)	20.5	14.0	11.0
Hull righting moment (ft.-lb.)	15,563.0*	8,300.0[†]	2,664.0[‡]
Mast capsizing moment (ft.-lb.)[§]	3,000.0	2,400.0	800.0
$A_s \times$ height to *CE*	4,305	3,080	2,607

* Of the total weight of 5,060 lb., the crew (nine men × 180 lb.) = 1,620 lb. and the boat = 3,440 lb. (one hull = 1,650 lb. and the beams = 140 lb.). Thus, the moments are, for one hull, 1,650 lb. × 5.25 ft. of beam = 8,663 ft.-lb.; for the crew, with six men on the gunwale, 1,080 lb. × 6 ft. = 6,480 ft.-lb.; and for half the weight of the beams, 70 lb. × 6 ft. = 420 ft.-lb.

[†] Moment is calculated as float (300 lb. × 12 ft. = 3,600 ft.-lb.) plus one man far out (180 lb. × 10 ft. = 1,800 ft.-lb.) plus two men out (360 lb. × 7 ft. = 2,520 ft.-lb.) plus beams (180 lb. × 6 ft. = 1,080 ft.-lb.) minus lee platform (200 lb. × 3.5 ft. = 700 ft.-lb.)

[‡] Moment is calculated as weather float weight plus lee float buoyancy ((54 lb. + 182 lb.) × 7 ft. = 1,652 ft.-lb.) plus three crew (440 lb. × 2.3 ft. = 1,012 ft.-lb.).

[§] Calculated as spar weights (200, 200, and 80 lb., respectively) times heights to centers of weights (15, 12, and 10 ft., respectively).

dine III, has Br = 1.18; and a modern offshore racing trimaran, *Manureva*, had Br = 1.44; Boehmer, 1979, p. 39). Speed is roughly proportional to the size of the Bruce number, so the expected performance ranking is double outrigger, 1; shunting single outrigger, 2; and double canoe, 3. A reasoned estimate would rank tacking outriggers higher than double canoes but lower than shunting single outriggers.

2C. Measured speeds of three existing canoes. In the real world, nonquantifiable factors enter into sailboat performance and modify the simple relationship of sail area divided by weight. The actual performance of three of the measured boats is indicated in Fig. 34, a polar diagram in which the ratio of boat speed (V_B) to true wind speed (V_T) is plotted against course angle away from true wind direction. It is obvious that *Nalehia* does not sail as fast as the other two boats, which have roughly comparable performance. *Mikael* sails better close-hauled because of more effective lateral resistance and a more efficient crane spritsail; *Nardi* makes more leeway and uses a rectangular boom lugsail with partially unsupported luff. Off the wind, however, the double outrigger outsails the single outrigger because of relatively larger sail (Br = 1.33) and probable lower skin friction. From

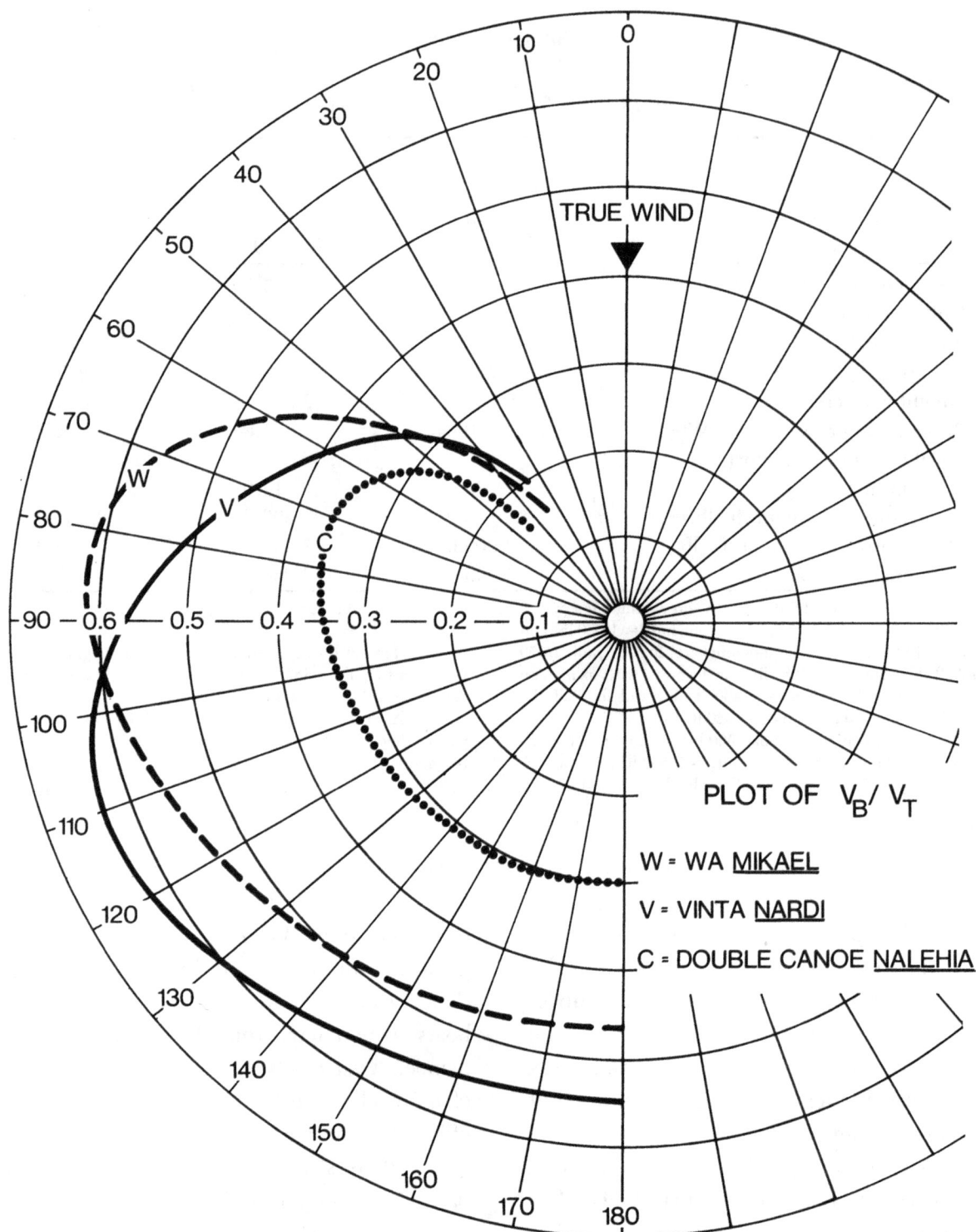

FIG. 34. Polar sailing diagram for three canoes. Boat speeds (expressed as the ratio between boat speed and true wind speed) are plotted for various course angles away from the true wind direction. For example, in a 10-knot wind the *vinta*, when making good a course 60° off the true wind, will sail at 4 knots; the *wa*, at 80° off the true wind, will sail at 6 knots.

these data a shared speed ranking of 1.5 for the two outriggers is indicated, and a ranking of 3 for the double canoe is obvious.

Note that the comparisons just made are not completely valid because of data constraints. Only *Mikael* is truly seagoing, whereas *Nalehia* and *Nardi* have relatively low freeboard and would not be used for long interisland voyages. *Hokule'a*, the sixty-two-foot double canoe which sailed from Hawaii to Tahiti and back in 1976 (Finney, 1977), is much larger than the other canoes and has incomplete performance data, two reasons for not using it as a double-canoe standard. Its Bruce number of 0.79 and its measured speeds only a bit higher than those for *Nalehia* make it unlikely that the speed ranking above would change if it were used as the example. No performance data whatsoever exist for double outriggers other than *Nardi* or for tacking single outriggers.

A design feature which clearly adds to the speed of some double-outrigger canoes should be noted despite the lack of distributional data which might permit inferences for culture history. In Sulu the long axes of both outrigger floats diverge outward (are toed out) from parallelism with the long axis of the main hull by any angle from 1° to 3.5° (note Fig. 17). As the canoe sails forward, close-hauled or on a reach, it makes considerable leeway. The main hull slides sideways slightly (has an angle of attack to the water equal to the leeway angle; see Fig. 19, upper diagram) and the drag on the hull is increased proportionately. In these, as in all double outrigger canoes, the weather float flies out of the water and does not contribute to drag except by air friction. The toed-out lee float's angle of attack is reduced from that of the main hull by the toe-out angle (angle of attack equals leeway angle minus toe-out angle), hence the drag on the float is much reduced and speed accordingly is enhanced. (See Doran, 1976, for data measured on a twenty-eight-foot double outrigger analogue with the float in three positions: toed in by 4°, parallel with the main hull, and toed out by 4°. The increase in speed as the float position changes, from toed in to parallel and then to toed out, is unmistakable.)

All double-outrigger canoes in Sulu are toed out at present (Doran, forthcoming), and one Makassar canoe is known to have toed-out floats (Johnson, 1974), but no other current data on this trait are available. When Admiral Paris reported on his survey of the 1830's, a curious partial distribution could be noted. Three canoes in the Philippines, in the vicinity of Manila, had floats which were toed in (Paris, 1841–1843, plates 70, 72, and 74), whereas one canoe in Java had toed-out floats (plate 91). Three canoes in Menado (northeastern Sulawesi) had floats parallel to the main hull (plates 97 and 100), as did a canoe in Amboina (plate 101), another in Waigeo (plate 104), and two canoes near Manokwari on Geelvink Bay (plates 104 and 105). In the absence of adequate present-day data, it would be unwise to do more than suggest that this trait should be recorded in future field work and that it might have some useful implications for culture history.

2D. Estimated speeds of three hypothetical canoes. Because of the data constraints mentioned above, it was decided to construct three hypothetical canoes of similar carrying capacity and then compare them. Insofar as possible, real-world characteristics of double canoes, single outriggers of the Micronesian type, and double outriggers were used as patterns. Most of the assumptions used will seem reasonable enough, but several will have to be justified.

The canoes will be assumed to be simple hollow cylinders, half submerged, with length-to-beam ratios of 16:1. Wall thickness will be taken as 1/16 the diameter, wetted surface as one-half the cylinder surface area, weight of the wood as 34 pounds per cubic foot, and weight of seawater as 64 pounds per cubic foot. From these assumptions, plus an initial length of forty feet for the double canoe, the data of Table 2 begin to emerge. For equal hull volumes the single-outrigger and double-outrigger canoes will be about fifty feet long with somewhat greater hull beams. Float dimensions of fifty feet long by one foot in diameter are a reasoned guess based on many dimensions recorded by Haddon and Hornell (1936–1938) plus my own field observations.

The most potentially controversial of all assumptions is that of widths from centerline to centerline: six feet, twenty-five feet, and forty feet, respectively, for the three configurations. The six-foot figure is approximately the same as that for *Nalehia* and conforms to narrow beams typical of Polynesian double canoes. An overall length twice the beam is found on many Micronesian canoes (for example, *Mikael*); hence, no great argument against the twenty-five-foot overall width on the hypothetical single outrigger seems likely. But the forty-foot width overall for the double outrigger is more dubious. Three smaller boats measured in the Philippines had ratios of overall length to overall beam of 1.8, 1.8, and 1.7, but a large 115-foot boat had beam practically

equal to length (Doran, forthcoming). The ratio of 1.25 used here seems reasonable in view of the large boat's dimensions.

Discounting crew and cargo weights, the maximum stability of each boat was obtained by multiplying beam times weight and/or bouyancy of float(s) or hull. Working backwards from maximum stability, it was determined that an equally large capsizing force would be reached at apparent wind speeds, respectively, of 22.9, 43.3, and 59.4 knots on the originally assumed 250-square-foot sail. Another way of stating much the same thing is to calculate the sail areas for each boat which would make righting and capsizing forces equal at 22.9 knots of apparent wind speed. Finally, from these last sail areas the respective Bruce numbers are obtained, and we find that they are in the same rank order as the Bruce numbers of the real-world boats of section 2B above. Note, however, that wetted surface, hence skin friction, is appreciably higher for the double outrigger if the single outrigger is assumed to fly its float out of water. Under these conditions the two boats might be about the same in speed.

A somewhat different picture emerges, however, if we assume all three craft to be loaded with five tons of crew and cargo. With half that weight in each hull, the stability of the double canoe becomes greater than that of the single outrigger, although still much lower than that of the double outrigger. Following the same procedure as above, we arrive at Bruce numbers for the double outrigger of 1.64; for the double canoe, 1.38; and for the single outrigger, 1.23. In other words, cargo weight improves the stability of the double canoe but does not improve that of outrigger canoes. Double canoes are better than single out-

TABLE 2. Comparison of Three Hypothetical Canoes.

Dimensions and Calculated Data	Double Canoe	Outrigger Canoe Hull	Float	Single Outrigger Complete	Double Outrigger Complete
Length (ft.)	40.0	50.0	50.0	50.0	50.0
Beam (ft.)	2.5	3.125	1.0	3.125	3.125
Wall thickness (ft.)	0.156	0.2		0.2	0.2
Inner-cylinder diameter (ft.)	2.188	2.73		2.73	2.73
Overall width, centerline to centerline (ft.)	6.0			25.0	40.0
Sail area, initial (sq. ft.)	250.0			250.0	250.0
Height to center of effort, CE, of sail (ft.)	21.0			21.0	21.0
Volume (displacement), 1 hull (cu. ft.)	196.35	383.50	39.27	422.77	462.04
Volume (displacement), 2 hulls (cu. ft.)	392.7				
Inner-cylinder volume (cu. ft.)	150.40	292.7			
Two-cylinder volume (cu. ft.)	300.8				
Wall volume (cu. ft.)	91.9	90.8			
Empty					
Weight (lb.)	3,124.6	3,087.2	1,335.2	4,422.4	5,757.6
Wetted surface (sq. ft.)	314.2	245.4	157.1	245.4	402.5
Maximum stability (ft.-lb.)	9,374.0			33,380.0	62,833.0
Apparent wind speed, V_A, at which hull or float lifts (knots)	22.9			43.3	59.4
Sail area to lift hull or float at 22.9 knots (sq. ft.)	250.0			892.0	1,681.0
Bruce number at 22.9 knots	1.08			1.82	2.29
Loaded					
Weight (lb.)	13,125			14,422	15,758
Maximum stability (ft.-lb.)	39,375			33,380	62,833
Sail area to lift hull or float at 22.9 knots (sq. ft.)	1,053			892	1,681
Bruce number at 22.9 knots	1.38			1.23	1.64

riggers as cargo vessels, but inferior to them in speed when light or empty of cargo, and both are inferior to double-outrigger canoes either light or loaded. A reasonable overall ranking on speed would be double outrigger 1 and the others with a shared ranking of 2.5.

I should emphasize here that the basic change in multihull design which produced faster boats to the west was an increase in beam which permitted a decrease in weight with the same stability. If double canoes had been beamier, they could have carried more sail safely, but the lashing materials and hull stress points could not have withstood the increased forces. The line in Table 2 which shows maximum stability (which is also a measure of forces that must be withstood) appears to be a contradiction, but another basic design change accommodates the increased force on the hull lashings. The shroud from masthead to float (see Fig. 30*B*) is in tension between float weight and wind capsizing force at the masthead and relieves much of the stress on crossbeam lashings of a single-outrigger canoe with its float to weather. And the bouyancy forces on the partially submerged lee float of a double outrigger (see Fig. 30*D*) are probably somewhat lower than the weight forces on the weather float, which also are sustained by a shroud. In other words, increase in beam on outrigger craft permitted stability and lashing forces of a similar order to those of double canoes but a significant reduction in weight. On empty boats of equal volume, the overall weight was greater for outrigger craft, but the increase in stability was far greater—hence the higher Bruce numbers.

3. *Use of Crew Weight for Increasing Stability.* Even in larger sizes, single-outrigger canoes used the weight of one or more members of the crew out toward the weather-side float (or, in Polynesia, on a weather-side balance board when the float was to leeward) to increase the stability moment. The exertion required and the exposure to the elements made it difficult to maintain a person or persons in such a position for more than a few hours. On a double canoe the crew might be mostly on or in the weather hull but were in more protected situations. The increased stability of double outriggers required little use of crew weight in exposed positions. The ranking based

on this rather significant aspect of long-distance voyaging would be double outrigger, 1; double canoe, 2; and single outrigger, 3.

4. *Rate of Capsize.* A fundamental aspect of seaworthiness lies in the rate at which a capsize takes place. If the rate is relatively slow, then preventive measures can be taken: crew weight can be shifted to weather, the boat can be luffed into the wind a bit, and the sheet can be slacked to lower the wind force on the sail. A rapid rate of capsize does not allow time for safety measures. Having sailed on primitive double canoes, single outriggers, and double outriggers as well as on modern catamarans, proas, and trimarans—not to mention having personally capsized the last two types and having watched many catamaran capsizes—I have a strong intuitive feeling for the capsize rates involved. Unfortunately, the physics of rigorous proof is beyond my capabilities. I shall make a qualitative attempt to establish a rank order among the three basic types and invite those with deeper understanding of the physics of sailing craft to verify or disprove my assertions.

It appears that rate of capsize is a function of two variables (which I have been unable to combine satisfactorily). The first of these, radial inertia, is a function of mass times radius squared. If we use the weights and overall widths of Table 2, the following data on radial inertia emerge for each of the canoe types:

Double canoe	$(13,125 \div 2) \times 6^2 =$	236,250 ft.-lb.
Single outrigger	$1,335 \times 25^2 =$	834,375 ft.-lb.
Double outrigger	$\approx 2(1,335 \times 25^2) =$	1,668,750 ft.-lb.

Based on inertia, clearly a function of rate, the

ranking is from bottom to top in these calculations.

The second variable depends on the relative densities of the two fluids (air and water) and the drag involved in moving either a hull or a float sideways through the fluid. The coefficient of drag for a long streamlined cylinder moved sideways instead of lengthwise through water is about ten times as great (Hoerner, 1965, pp. 10–13); hence, in the first place we are dealing with a high-drag object. Second, the density of water is about eight hundred times that of air, so the rate of an object moving through water necessarily must be lower by a very considerable amount than its rate when moving through air. (Note in Figs. 30C and D that the float will submerge before the main hull can lift from the water.)

A point which I am unable to demonstrate rigorously but know from experience is that there is a very large difference between the capsize rates of the canoes in Figs. 30A and B on the one hand and Figs. 30C and D on the other. Using the above approximations and referring to Fig. 30A, we can see that a double canoe capsize involves a relatively low moment of inertia and movement of the weather hull through air, a low-density medium, so a double canoe has a high rate of capsize. A single-outrigger canoe with float to weather (Fig. 30B) would have a greater moment of inertia (because of much greater beam despite the lower weight of the float) and the same density relationship as a double canoe, hence a somewhat lower rate of capsize. A single outrigger with float to leeward (Fig. 30C) has the same moment of inertia as the canoe of Fig. 30B, but the float must be depressed through a fluid of much higher density, so the canoe will have a far slower rate of capsize.

The double-outrigger canoe (Fig. 30D) combines the forces of Figs. 30B and C; hence, it has an even slower rate of capsize than that of the single outrigger in Fig. 30C. There is ample time to take corrective measures after a modern trimaran submerges its lee float, but a proa with float to weather, particularly running nearly downwind, capsizes with lightning speed.

The rank order, then, is double outrigger, 1; single outrigger, 2; and double canoe, 3.

5. *Sail Balance*. When a vessel is sailing at constant speed, there must be an equilibrium between the propulsive force (considered to be focused at the center of effort of the sail) and an equal and opposite resistance force centered on the hull's center of resistance. If these two forces lie along or close to a straight line, sail balance has been achieved. But if the two forces are parallel but offset from each other, there is introduced a couple, a tendency for the vessel to turn away from its course. This tendency must be counteracted by the steering mechanism, introducing more drag and slowing the vessel. Under extreme conditions the vessel becomes uncontrollable. Most Austronesian canoes have reasonably good sail balance built into their design, but Polynesian single outrigger canoes are badly out of balance on one tack. Fig. 35 shows that double canoes (A) and double-outrigger canoes (D) have good balance, as do Micronesian single outriggers (C) because of the movement of the sail from one end of the boat to the other in shunting. On the tack in which the float is to windward (normally the port tack), Polynesian single outriggers (B) have good balance, but the balance is badly off on the other tack. This lack of balance on one tack is very likely another of the principal reasons that large voyag-

⇓ WIND ⇓

 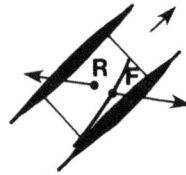 A. Polynesian Double Canoe

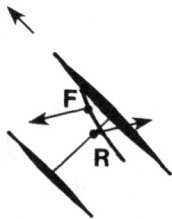 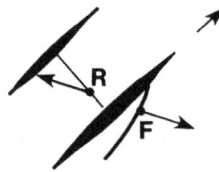 B. Polynesian Single Outrigger

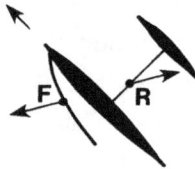  C. Micronesian Single Outrigger

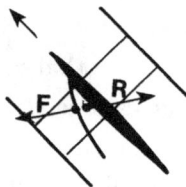 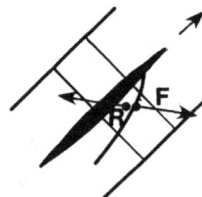 D. Indonesian Double Outrigger

Starboard Tack   Port Tack

F=Force

R=Resistance

FIG. 35. Sail balance in four canoe configurations.

ing canoes in Polynesia were typically double canoes instead of single outriggers. Once the shunting technique of achieving sail balance by moving the sail from one end of the canoe to the opposite (plus the desirable factor of keeping the float always to weather) was invented, the need for double canoes diminished. Shunting single outriggers were not only easier to build but also used fewer materials and were far faster than double canoes. The nearly total disappearance of double canoes in Micronesia and Melanesia, where all canoes are shunted, is probably in part a reflection of these implications of sail balance. Because only tacking single outriggers are inferior, sail balance is not included as a ranking, but the considerations above must be kept in mind in final assessment.

SUMMARY

In eight aspects of seaworthiness there is little significant difference among the three configurations of multihulled craft found in the Pacific. It must be emphasized again that all three are basically seaworthy, as the voyaging evidence for all types demonstrates. Particularly emphatic recognition must be given to the family similarity in stability curves for all Pacific canoes. The forgiving nature of multihulls, caused by the flattening or reversal of stability curves as the vessels heel to a sudden squall, must have saved countless lives through the millennia and must be included as one of the factors which made possible the known voyages across the reaches of the Pacific.

Another five aspects of seaworthiness, however, have been examined and reveal significant differences among the different kinds of Pacific craft. Because of lack of data, tacking single-outrigger canoes are not included in the summary. They must have shown a good turn of speed with float to weather but must have required crew balance weight to sail on either tack. The lack of sail balance must have made them very difficult to

TABLE 3. Summary of Seaworthiness Rankings.

Seaworthiness Component	Double Outrigger		Shunting Single Outrigger		Double Canoe	
1. Hull construction		1.00		2.50		2.50
2A. Speed, historical	1.5		1.5		3.0	
2B. Speed, real canoes, estimate	1.0		2.0		3.0	
2C. Speed, real canoes, measured	1.5		1.5		3.0	
2D. Speed, hypothetical, estimated	1.0		2.5		2.5	
2. Speed, average		1.25		1.88		2.88
3. Use of crew weight		1.00		3.00		2.00
4. Rate of capsize		1.00		2.00		3.00
Sum of rankings		4.25		9.38		10.38

handle, and for this reason alone they can be ranked as inferior to double canoes. The rankings for the other three types are totaled in Table 3.

I recognize, of course, that rankings are only crude approximations and that a boat ranked 1 is not necessarily twice as good as a boat ranked 2. In addition there is no way of comparing such factors as average speed and rate of capsize. Each will be more important as circumstances vary.

There do seem to be measurable differences among the different configurations, however. Least good are tacking single outriggers, whereas the undoubtedly good double canoes of Polynesia are outranked by the better shunting single outriggers of Micronesia and Melanesia, and these, in turn, by the best configuration, the double-outrigger canoes of Indonesia.

PREMISE AND HYPOTHESIS

Although examples of retrogression and loss of culture traits can be cited, there is agreement that cultures generally progress and that in technology the progression is cumulative (Kroeber, 1948, p. 303). In full awareness of the possibility of error, it will be taken as a basic assumption that where two cultures are in contact, both possessing items of similar function (in this case watercraft), the technically superior item will gradually replace the technically inferior item. At a given location the item which is replaced is probably older than the item which replaces it. Based on this reasoning as applied to seaworthiness, a hypothesis of relative ages of multihulled watercraft in the Pacific can be developed.

If the seaworthiness of watercraft ranges from good through better to best in the east-west direction from Polynesia through Micronesia and

Melanesia to Indonesia, then it follows that age relationships should range from oldest in the east through intermediate in the central area to youngest in the west. It has been demonstrated above that the most seaworthy watercraft are the double outriggers of Indonesia; hence, these are most likely to be the youngest type. Single outriggers of Micronesia and Melanesia are intermediate in location, efficiency, and age, and the double canoes (and tacking single outriggers) of Polynesia, seaworthy as they undoubtedly are, are less so than craft to the west and therefore are presumed to be the oldest canoe types in the Pacific.

From this hypothesis of age relationships based on analysis of seaworthiness we now can proceed to an examination of the distributions of boat traits and of estimates about ages which can be inferred in turn from them.

6

The Distributional Evidence

~~~~~~

IT is a truism that nonrandom distributions of objects or traits in space reflect the physical or cultural processes (and perhaps sequence of processes) which have affected the objects or traits. If the processes or their sequences are poorly understood, sometimes it is possible to understand them better by thinking backward logically from the distributions they have affected. In Austronesia before World War II there were essentially no absolute dates from historic records and no relative dates from stratigraphic excavations. The only dating techniques available were the use of islanders' genealogies and the age-area hypothesis. Genealogies were suspect not only because of imprecision of human memories (in the absence of writing) but also because of post-European corruptions. The age-area hypothesis was an attempt to infer logical time relationships from known present-day space relationships.

In its most simplistic form, the age-area hypothesis (used first by paleontologists and biologists and later by anthropologists) assumed that an innovation starting at a given point would move outward by diffusion from group to group in radial directions. A later innovation at the same point also would radiate outward but behind the first innovation because of its later date of origin.

Subsequent innovations would form smaller concentric circles as of any given time, and ages could be inferred as decreasing from the periphery (the first innovation) back toward the center of innovation. Flaws in this simplistic hypothesis were quickly noted; because of obstacles (physical or cultural), ideas do not radiate outward at the same speed in all radii of the circle. Some traits are accepted faster than others and it is entirely conceivable that a later idea will go farther, in less time, than an earlier idea and be found on the periphery of the outermost circle. Despite these logical objections, the hypothesis, when carefully used, was of some value in working out problems of relative time.

With the advent of relative dating by use of stratified archaeological sites, of absolute dating by means of radiocarbon (and less accurately by glottochronology), and of increased emphasis on local ecological cause-and-effect relationships as explanation, the rather crude age-area hypothesis with its concomitant emphasis on diffusion as explanation has come into considerable disfavor. Nevertheless, there are problems, and understanding the culture history of watercraft in Austronesia is one, for which cautious use of the age-area hypothesis is a useful procedure because archaeological descriptions and dates are so sparse. The double-outrigger craft carved on the walls of the great temple at Boro Bodur in Java are long known (see Haddon, 1920, for line drawings of five of the seven craft) and give a useful date of about A.D. 800. Recent excavations by Sinoto at Huahine, Society Islands, have uncovered parts of what is probably a double canoe, radiocarbon-dated at A.D. 780–1270, with some doubt expressed about the dates (Emory, 1979, pp. 203–204). These, the dugouts found in Niah caves in Borneo (Johnstone 1980, p. 213), and three boats excavated from a river delta in Mindanao (Peralta, 1980) are all that we have at present. Because wooden materials are preserved in the hot and wet tropics only rarely, buried in mud under reducing conditions, and because most canoes in difficulty probably broke up but did not sink, we cannot expect much direct archaeological assistance on problems of canoe origins for a long time to come.

We will analyze the distribution maps which follow as carefully as possible, drawing any inferences which seem logical but always within the time framework established by radiocarbon dating of all types of artifacts and the best use of glottochronological estimates. Age-area dating, however, is the principal tool used in this chapter. A few of the maps have been taken from other sources with little modification, but most have been largely or completely recompiled for this book. Map sources are indicated on the maps themselves and in Appendix 1.

Although bark boats and wood or bamboo rafts lie outside our principal focus, it may be proper to begin with these two simplest types of watercraft in the Pacific. Although there is no firm evidence whatsoever, it seems reasonable to argue typologically that such simple craft, requiring nothing beyond the most primitive Stone Age tool kit, are the oldest craft of the region. If anything, rafts appear to be the simplest, and hence most likely the oldest. Distributions, however, suggest that bark boats are older (Figs. 36 and 37). The simplest of several types of bark boat is found in the interior of southeastern Australia (Fig. 38), where the oldest human remains have been dated as more than thirty thousand years old (Barbetti and Allen, 1972; Birdsell, 1977, p. 118). More complex tied bark boats are found along the coast of New South Wales, and still more complex ones farther to the north in Queensland and west of the Gulf of Carpentaria (Davidson, 1935, p. 80). Age-area dating and typology suggest decreasing age toward the north. The few examples of bark boats in Indonesia may represent relics from Old Melanesia (Fig. 26) and suggest that the earliest water crossings were made in similar craft. From their more limited and northward distribution in Australia (toward the original source), wood rafts seem to be a later introduction; the remainder of the distribution, Angola to the Tuamotus, suggests great age but continued utility. Archaeology tells us that the part of the distribution from the New Hebrides eastward must be only a few thousand years old, but the mainland Asiatic part may be of great antiquity. The crude, quickly saturated bark rafts of Tasmania, despite their peripheral location, need not invalidate the conclusion above. Unseaworthy and never used to cross distances greater than about eight miles (Jones, 1977, pp. 322–329), these rafts perhaps represent a retrogression in technology from bark boats.

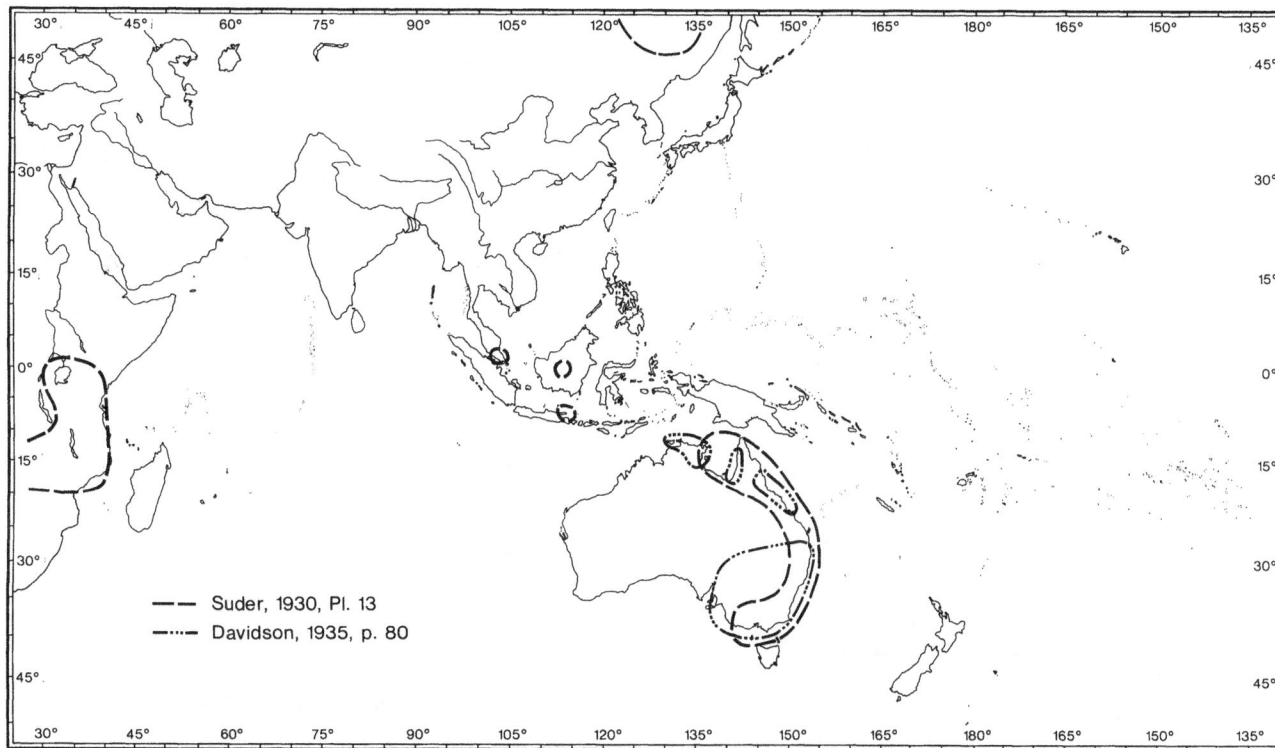

Fig. 36. Distribution of bark boats.

Suder, 1930, Pl. 13
Davidson, 1935, p. 80

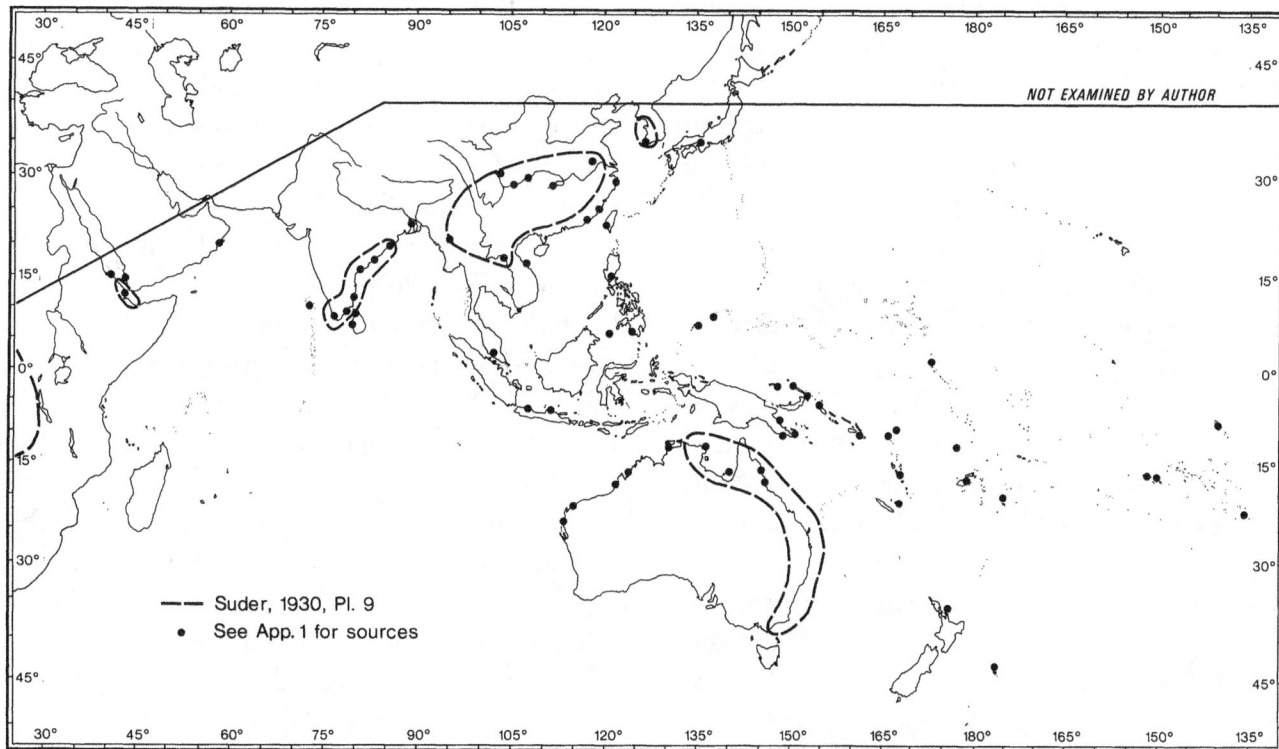

Fig. 37. Distribution of wood or bamboo rafts.

NOT EXAMINED BY AUTHOR

Suder, 1930, Pl. 9
See App. 1 for sources

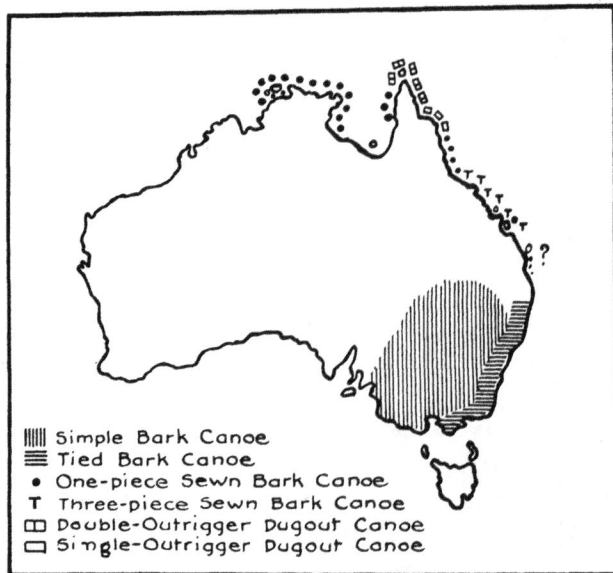

FIG. 38. Distribution of bark boats and outrigger canoes in Australia.

The very wide distribution of dugouts or log boats, across the forested parts of Africa and northern Eurasia and from India and China eastward into the Pacific, requires cautious interpretation by the age-area hypothesis (Fig. 39). An extent much greater than that of bark boats and rafts represents not greater age but more likely an extensive and continued use of a more efficient type of craft. Fragile and wet craft have been replaced in considerable measure by sturdier and drier boats, despite the much increased labor involved in their production. The continuous distribution from India to China and Japan and from mainland southeast Asia eastward into the Pacific suggests considerable age and continued utility despite the presence of later and more efficient boat types. The dugouts in northern Australia are known to be relatively recent Malay introductions (Davidson, 1935, p. 76) and thus younger than bark boats or rafts. Dugouts are still used in considerable numbers throughout Indonesia and New Guinea, but eastward of the Solomons the basic dugout hull must be stabilized by an outrigger or by doubling to meet open-water conditions. Retrogression from double canoes to the simple dugout in New Zealand is well documented and an exception to the general rule. On one point, that dugouts must have preceded both double canoes and outrigger canoes, there can be no doubt; the basic hull must have existed before it could be doubled or before appendages could be added.

We now turn to the inferences about the relative ages of double canoes, single-outrigger canoes, and double-outrigger canoes that we can make from distributions (Figs. 40–42). It is generally accepted that the original location from which Austronesian folk spread is somewhere in the Southeast Asian mainland or islands (see Fig. 29). If we take this region as the center of innovation, the earliest ideas for stabilizing long and narrow dugouts were the double canoe and single-outrigger canoe, ideas which spread far eastward to the limits of Polynesia, where they have been maintained as the principal boat types to the present (Figs. 40 and 41). A later innovation, the double-outrigger canoe, has started from about the same area but spread eastward a much shorter distance (Fig. 42).

A second implication of the maps is that the double canoe is somewhat older than the single-outrigger canoe. Fig. 40 shows a chain of double-canoe relicts leading back from Polynesia through Melanesia and Indonesia to the mainland, where double-canoe (or double-junk) relicts are to be found all the way from India to China. If the double canoe was first used on the mainland, it must

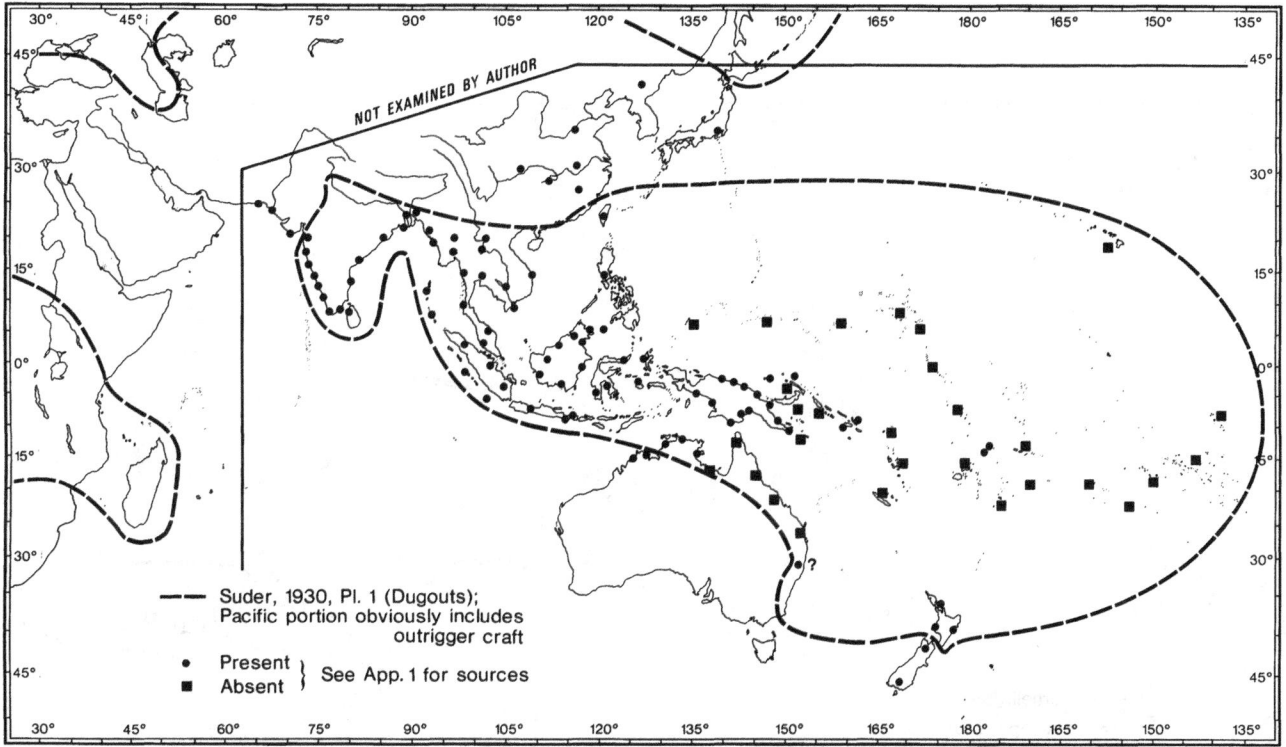

FIG. 39. Distribution of dugout canoes without outriggers.

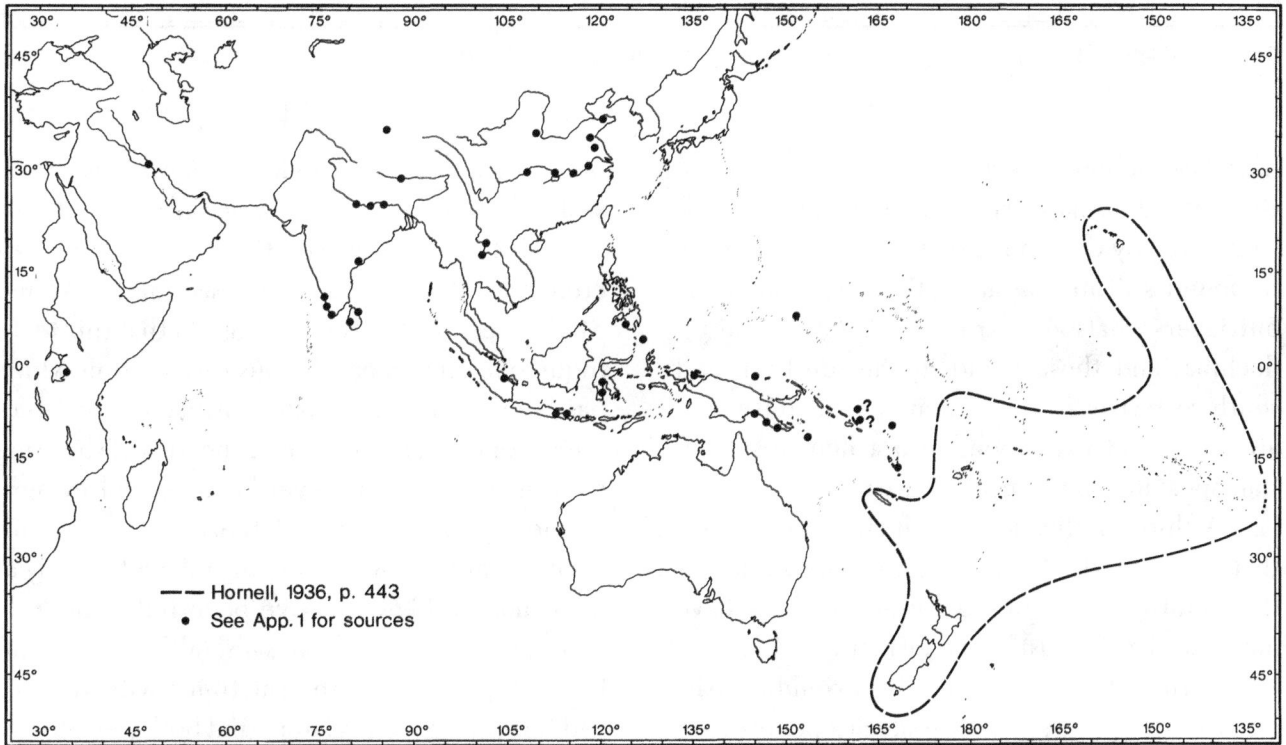

FIG. 40. Distribution of double canoes.

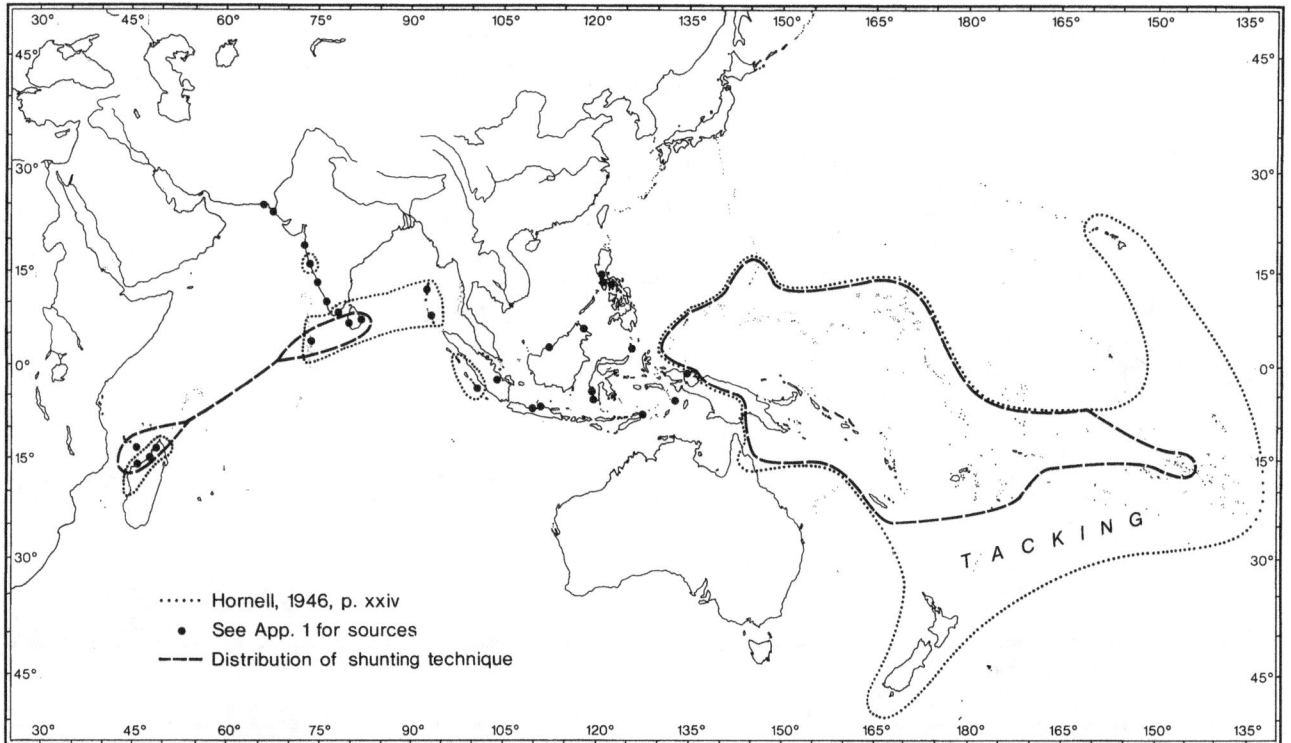

FIG. 41. Distribution of single-outrigger canoes and of shunting technique.

have been followed relatively soon by the invention in Indonesia of the single-outrigger canoe (suggested by the many relict single outriggers to be found still in that area [Fig. 41]). No single outriggers whatsoever are found in China and Indochina, and those found in the southern and southwestern coasts of India are postulated as relatively recent expansions into a non-Austronesian-speaking and Caucasoid area.

A third implication is that single outriggers that tack are older than single outriggers that use the shunting technique because the latter have not moved as far east as the former (see Fig. 41). The curious tongue of shunting extending east into the Tuamotus suggests eastward penetration

of the idea. Some hard evidence for this assertion will be noted when we examine sail distributions.

This disjunct distribution of shunting—Micronesia and Melanesia to the east, Sri Lanka and Madagascar to the west—suggests that this technique once had a continuous distribution which has been broken by a later intrusion of double-outrigger canoes. Not only is the idea of shunting so strange that it has never been used elsewhere in the world, but as well there are other similarities between Micronesian and Sri Lankan canoes most unlikely to have been independently invented. Both use spritsails (although of different types), both steer at times with quarter rudders (more on this later), and both seem to use

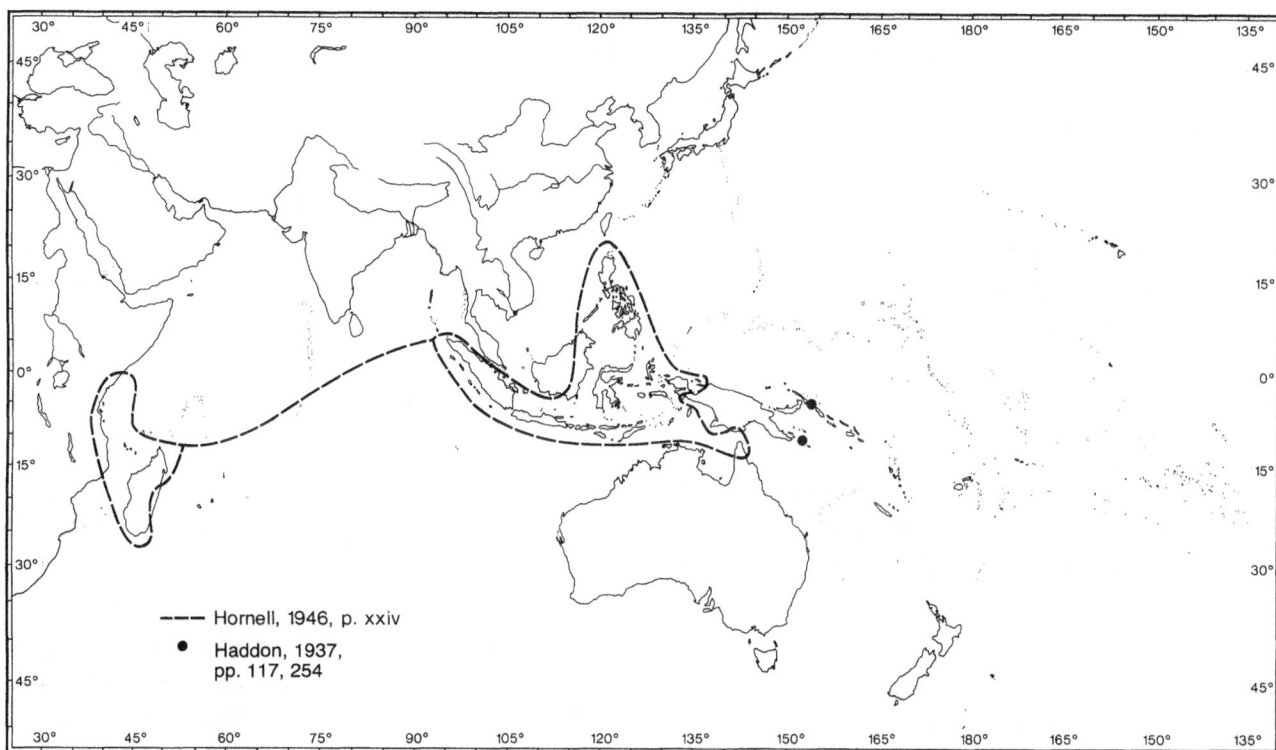

FIG. 42. Distribution of double-outrigger canoes.

a technique of steering when close-hauled by means of the sheet of the sail. (The technique is well known in Micronesia and probable but unproven for Sri Lanka.) To bear off the wind, the sail is pulled in a bit, thus shifting the direction of wind force aft and changing the sail balance into an offwind couple. Slacking the sheet does the reverse and brings the head closer to the wind because of outrigger drag. (This technique is exactly the opposite of that used by modern yachtsmen, who harden in on the sheet a bit to luff into the wind. See Fig. 35 on sail balance.) These unusual characteristics common to canoes in Micronesia and Sri Lanka make it very likely that they once had an uninterrupted distribution across Indonesia.

The outrigger evidence from the Cape York peninsula of Australia also points to single-outrigger canoes gradually being displaced southward along the Queensland coast by double-outrigger canoes and thus a younger age for the latter in this area, at least (Davidson, 1935, pp. 15, 71).

The distributional evidence is ambiguous in at least two instances. The great area of double-outrigger canoes along the east coast of Africa and in Madagascar might be taken as an implication of greater age. As we have seen, this point plus a typological argument plus some historical evidence persuaded Hornell of the greater age for double outriggers (1920*b*). Two counter-suggestions would explain the discrepancy. An earlier small migration in shunting single outriggers could have been mostly smothered by a larger and later invasion using double outriggers. Again, a recognized greater efficiency of double outriggers could have caused replacement of less efficient single outriggers over most of the East African coast (as presumably double outriggers replaced single outriggers in Indonesia).

A final small point is the two disjunct occurrences of double-outrigger canoes in Nissan and the Louisiades just southeast of New Guinea (Fig. 42). Although these occurrences could be considered relicts of a once larger distribution, I think it more likely that they represent long-distance colonization which took effect at these two points. We know that movements eastward along both the north and south sides of New Guinea were taking place when Europeans appeared on the scene (Great Britain, Admiralty, 1944*a*, p. 65; Lewthwaite, 1967, pp. 58–59; Forrest, 1780, p. 112), and they might well have extended somewhat farther eastward to the two points in question. Sail distributions also suggest such movements.

The sum of the distributional inferences based on hull types produces an age sequence as follows:

Youngest
Double outriggers
Single outriggers (shunted)
Single outriggers (tacked)
Double canoes
Dugouts
Rafts of wood or bamboo
Bark boats
Rafts of bark
Oldest

Our examination of the distributions of sails begins with a puzzling type, the double spritsail, which most observers have considered quite primitive despite its association with shunting canoes in Sri Lanka, the Maldive Islands, and Madagascar (Fig. 43). Another example, located vaguely "in Sumatra," is known from a model, with hull configuration indicating that it probably was tacked. The fifth example was noted in the early nineteenth century on an Arab vessel in the Red Sea. After much reflection I have come to believe that the presumed simplicity and primitiveness are deceptive and that the sail represents an early but sophisticated attempt to devise a rig which will permit shunting. Without shifting the spars, the clew of the sail (after corner) becomes the tack (forward corner) on the other shunt, and a simple way of moving the center of effort of the sail has been developed. Micronesian crane sprit technique is more efficient once the sail is shifted, but requires a more cumbersome rig to achieve the same end. The Indian Ocean distribution, probably associated with relatively late migration(s) to Madagascar, also tends to make one dubious about great age for the sail.

The next three sail types, Oceanic sprit, crane sprit, and boom lug, may be taken as a group because in broad terms they correlate very well with hull types. The Oceanic sprit (Fig. 44) is used on double canoes and tacking single outriggers (Figs. 40 and 41), the crane sprit (Fig. 45) is the sail rig for most shunting single outriggers (Fig. 41), and the boom-lug sail (Fig. 46) correlates closely with double-outrigger canoes (Fig. 42). What are likely to be relicts of earlier use of the Oceanic sprit are found in the central New Hebrides and scattered locations in islands west-

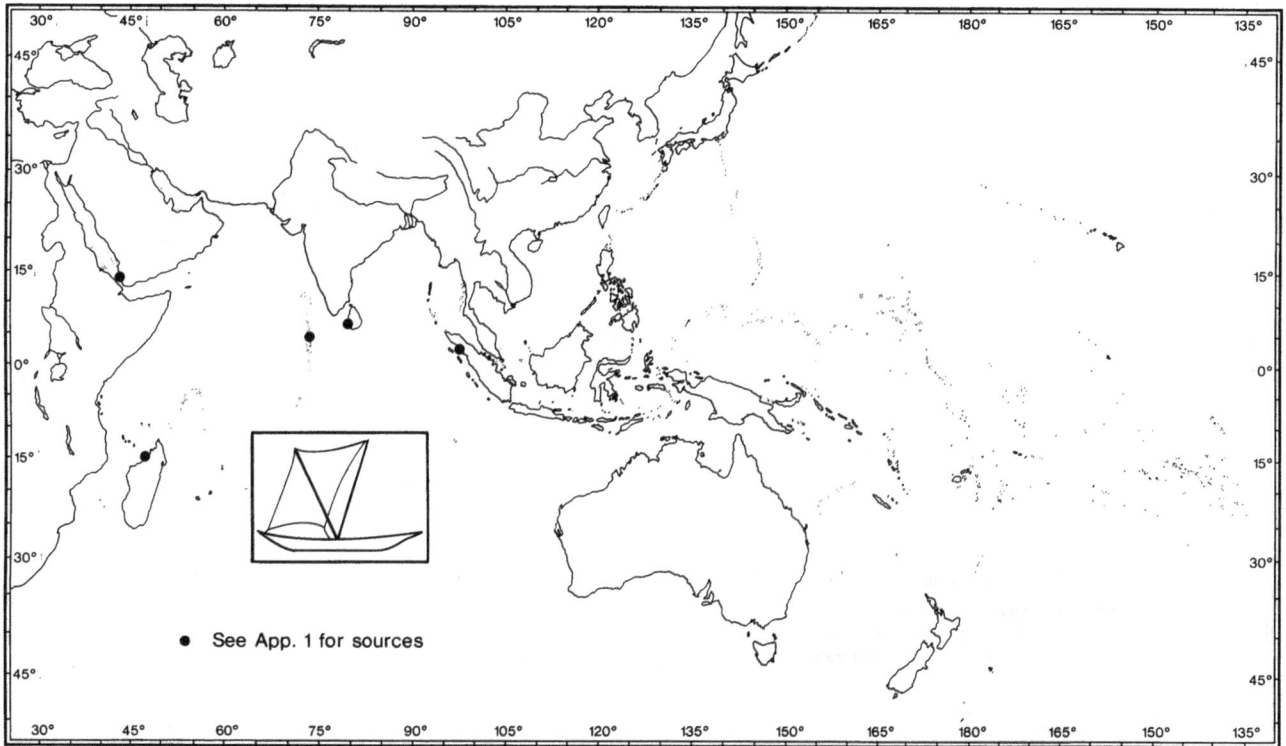

FIG. 43. Distribution of the double spritsail.

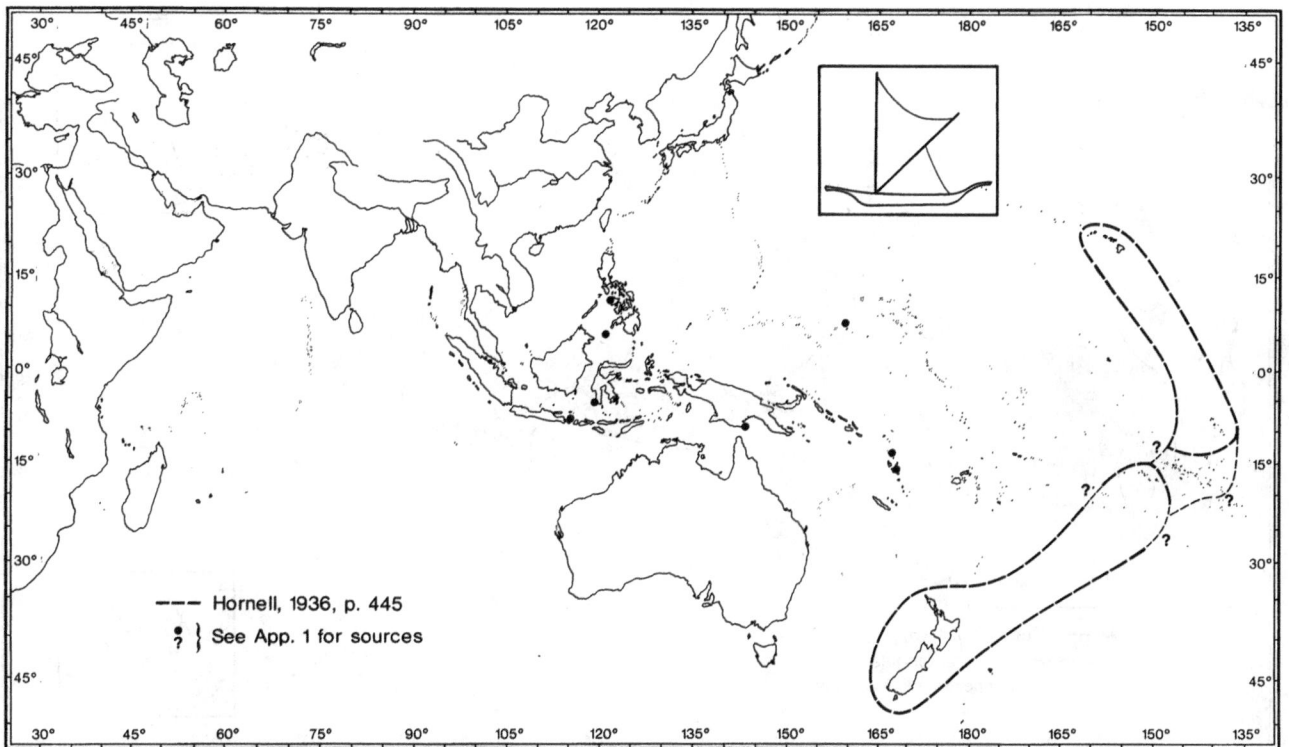

FIG. 44. Distribution of the Oceanic spritsail.

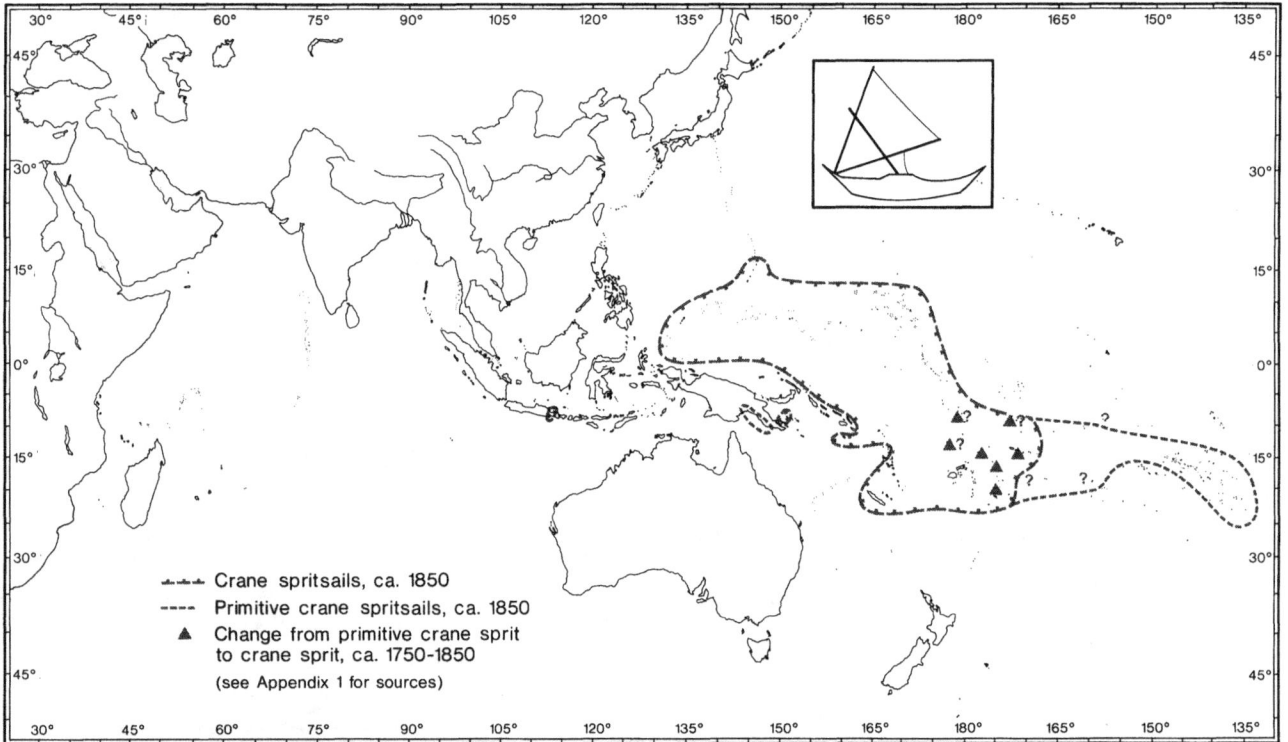

FIG. 45. Distribution of the crane spritsail and primitive crane spritsail.

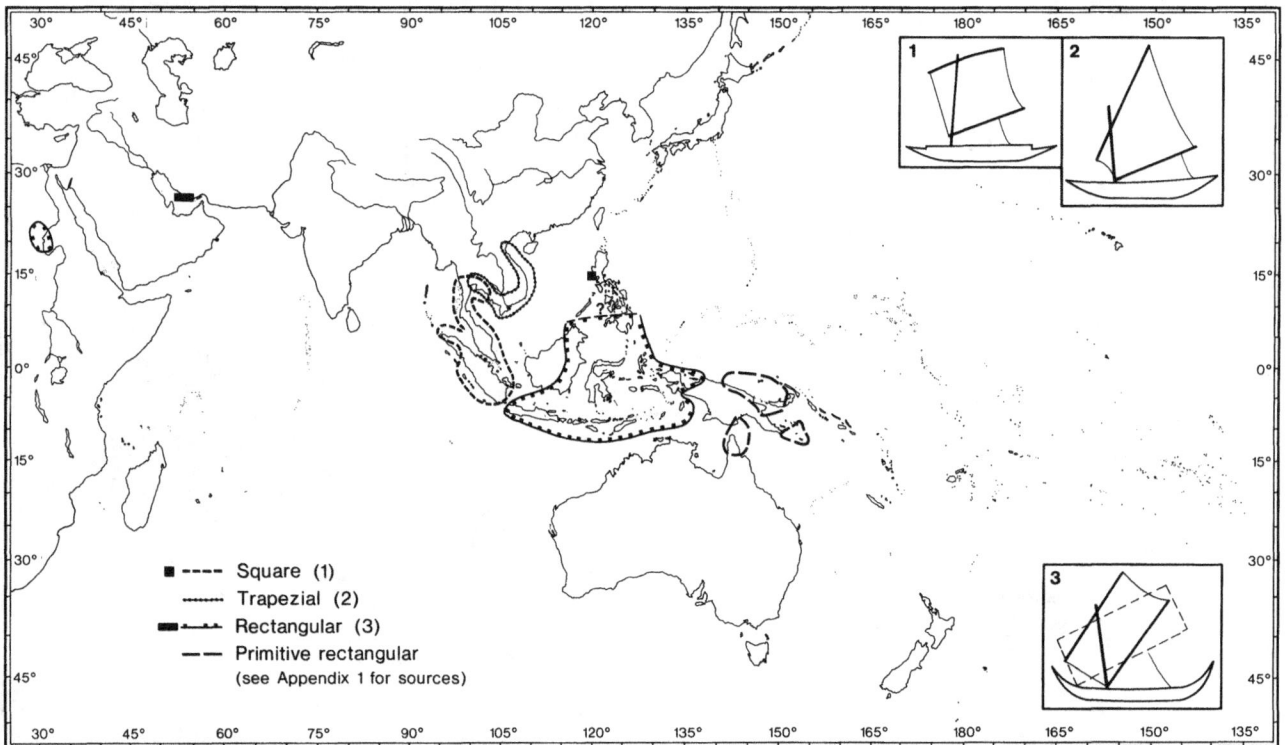

FIG. 46. Distribution of boom lugsails.

ward to Indonesia. Presumed relicts of the crane sprit are found in East Java. But the most important firm evidence concerns the known expansion eastward, between 1600 and 1800, of the crane spritsail and shunting. Early seventeenth-century explorers such as Schouten and Tasman found primitive crane sprits and tacking in use in Tonga, and Cook found the changeover to crane sprits and shunting in process (Hornell, 1936, p. 265). There is no question that the ideas were moving eastward at that point, and there is a high degree of probability that shunting and primitive crane sprits in the Tuamotus were part of the same process. Age-area reasoning and hypotheses about sails, then, are exactly the same as those discussed for hull types. Oceanic spritsails are earliest and spread eastward with the Polynesians. Crane spritsails are somewhat younger, principally associated with shunting canoes in Micronesia and Melanesia but actively spreading eastward and replacing Oceanic spritsails. Boom lugsails are least in area, closest to the center of dispersion of Austronesians, and thus the youngest of the three types.

Other useful inferences may be drawn from the distribution of the several types of boom lugsails (Fig. 46). Sources are adequate to map the several types with reasonable accuracy except in the Philippines, where data are incomplete. No rectangular boom lugsails have been found north of the A.D. 1500 Moro line through Mindanao (shown as the north limit on the map) and only two square boom lugs are known. Most abundant are common spritsails (discussed below) plus a cosmopolitan mixture in Manila (see sources for Fig. 46 in Appendix 1).

We have already seen that the typological sequence from trapezial to square to rectangular boom lugsails has long been noted and the distribution hinted at. The accurate mapping (except for the Philippines) of the three types plus recognition of a fourth in the typological sequence, primitive rectangular lugs, makes possible more precise inferences, especially if modern sail theory is used to infer relative efficiencies of the four types.

In brief, efficiency declines from trapezial to square to rectangular to primitive boom lug (see Figs. 21 and 24). The trapezial boom lug has a higher aspect ratio (greater height to width) and pointed peak which reduce induced drag in the same way that modern high-aspect-ratio yacht sails do. The very short luff is more efficient than the longer luffs on the other sails, and the sail simply swings across in tacking, again as in modern sails. The square lug is not quite as good as the rectangular lug from the standpoint of aspect ratio, but the small area forward of the mast again permits the sail to swing across simply when tacking. The rectangular lug has much area forward of the mast—a long, unsupported luff—and must be shifted to the lee side on each tack, either by dipping or by rolling up the sail, passing it around the mast, and then unrolling it on the new lee side. The primitive lugs have very high centers of effort and low aspect ratios, both deleterious, but swing around easily as the canoe shunts to the new tack.

Distribution of the four sails, then, is a typological cline from Vietnam to Malaya and Sumatra, to the remainder of Indonesia, and then to Melanesia. The same cline exists from the standpoint of efficiency, and one may hypothesize that the center of innovation has been in Indochina,

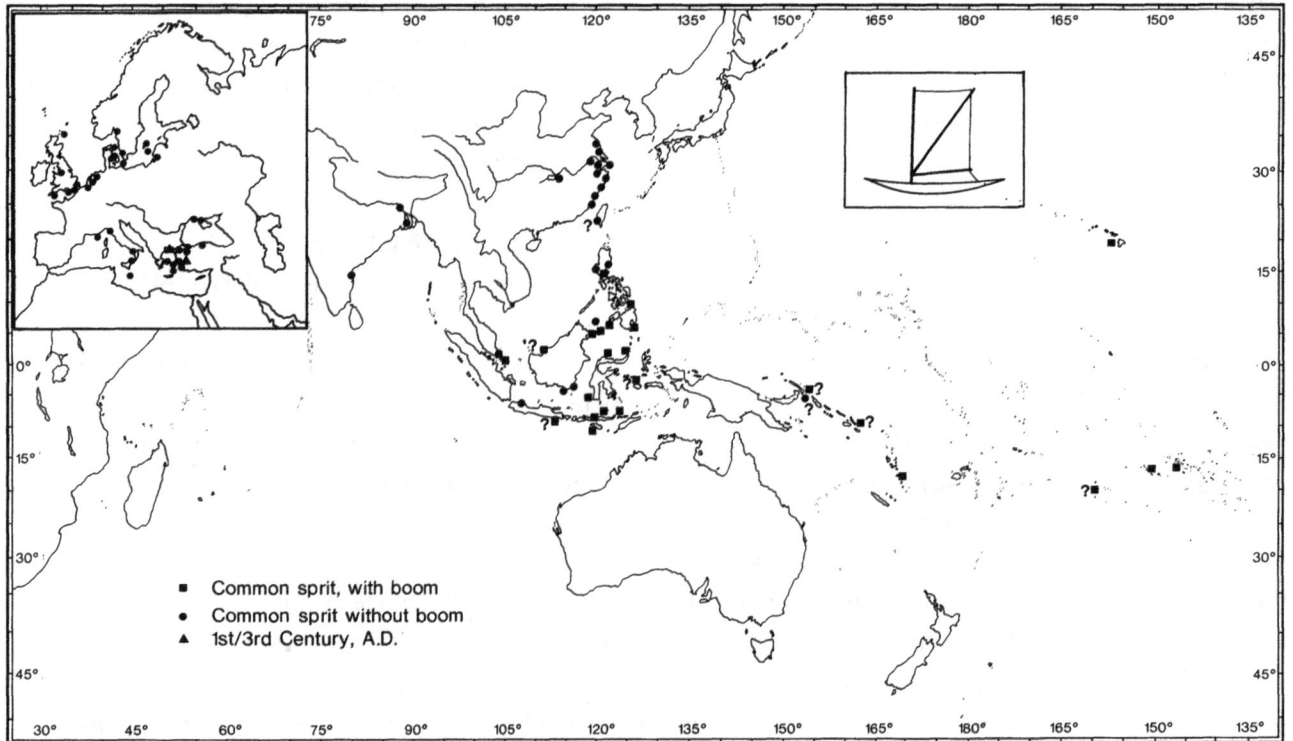

FIG. 47. Distribution of the common spritsail.

with ideas and improvements flowing south, then east. The most primitive (and oldest) form of the sail lies in Melanesia, and the types found westward and then northward into Indochina are progressively younger. Note that the sail's eastward movement is presumably much later than the original dispersal of Austronesian horticulturists.

The puzzling distribution of the common spritsail is included for two reasons (Fig. 47). The scattered distribution eastward in the Pacific and concentrated distribution from Chekiang and Fukien in China straight southward through the Philippines and Indonesia to islands east of Java may prove to be useful evidence as the culture history of Indonesia becomes known in more detail. The good correlation between distributions of the common spritsail with boom and the word *katig* for outrigger float (Haddon, 1920, p. 119) suggests a cultural connection which predates the spread of the boom lug considered above. *Katig* is cognate with the proto-Austronesian reconstruction for outrigger float, whereas *sama* and its cognates for float are reconstructed for the proto-Oceanic language (Bismarcks area) and for proto–Central Pacific still farther east (Pawley and Green, 1975, p. 34). We have already associated tacking single outriggers, using Oceanic spritsails, with proto-Austronesian. Moderately early modification from Oceanic spritsails to common spritsails is at least a possibility. Occurrences

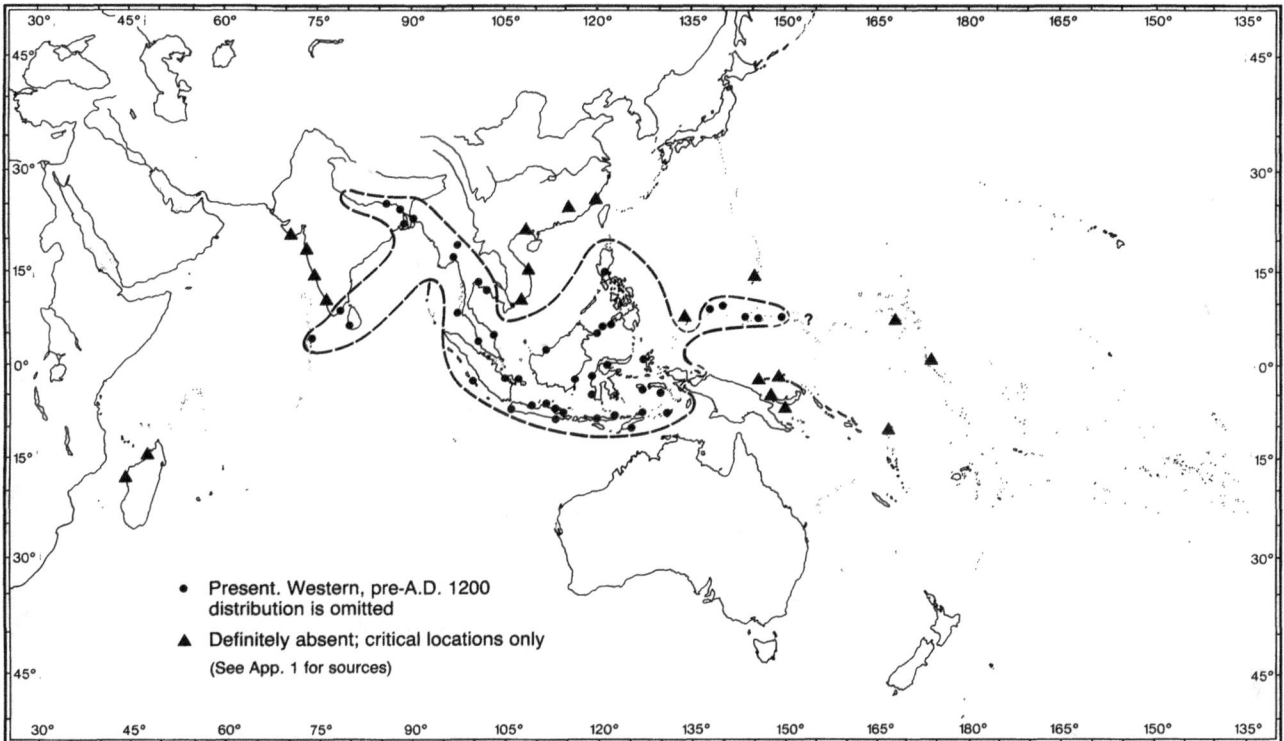

FIG. 48. Distribution of the quarter rudder.

eastward of Indonesia are considered to be post-European introductions.

The two European distributions are included in the inset of Fig. 47 because we have dates for them which might prove indirectly useful. Common spritsails without booms appear in northwestern Europe early in the fifteenth century (Phillips-Birt, 1962, p. 76) and for a long time were thought to have been invented by the Dutch. The eastern Mediterranean distribution and Casson's discovery of Roman-period spritsails (second and third centuries A.D.) moved the spritsail back in European history for more than a millennium (Casson, 1971, figs. 147, 175, 176 and 177–179) and aroused speculation about an East-

ern origin for the sail type (Bowen, 1959, p. 157). An introduction from the Far East during the period of Graeco-Roman contacts with India and Han China is a possibility and gives a very crude date for existence of the sail in Indonesia.

Two more Austronesian boat traits may have some value in untangling the region's culture history. The quarter rudder, a steering device attached to the vessel's quarter (back "corner") instead of its stern, has the distribution shown in Fig. 48. In China we know of the existence of the stern rudder from the first century A.D. (Needham, 1971, p. 650), and all vessels southward in Annam use stern rudders. Quarter rudders were in use in the West from earliest Egyptian times,

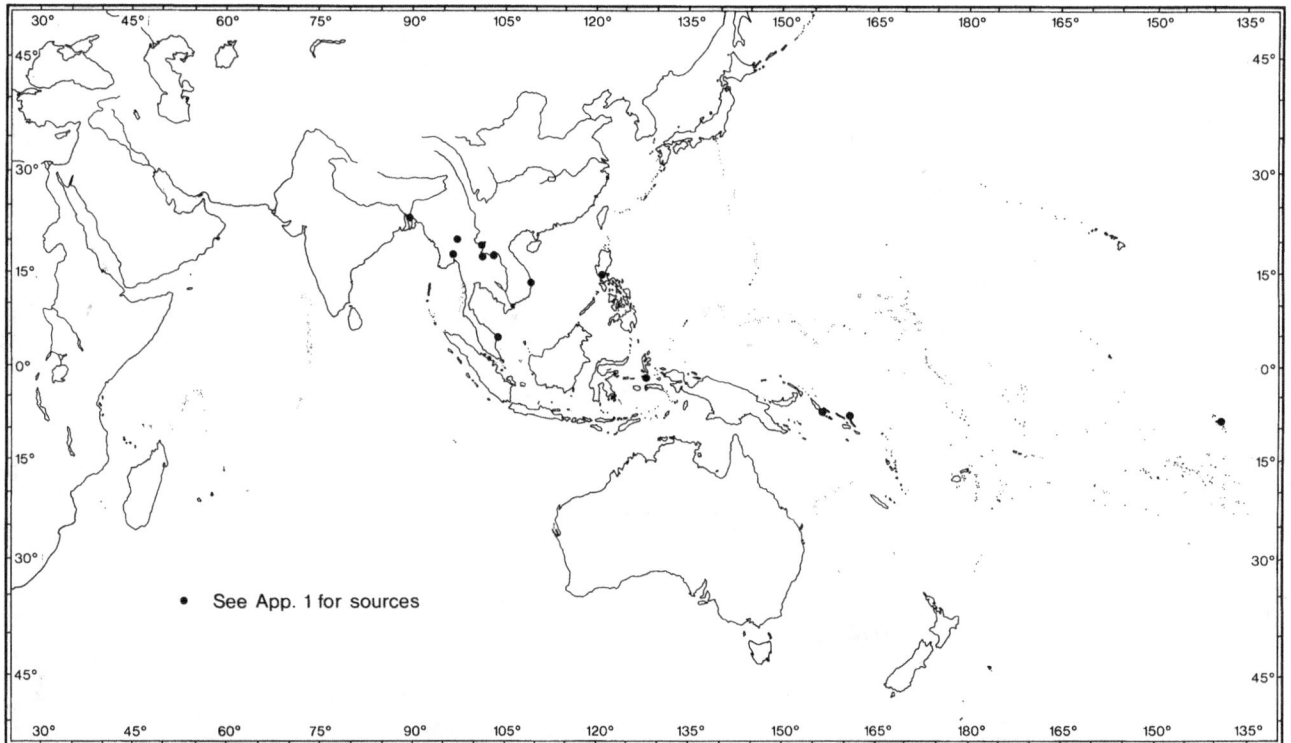

FIG. 49. Distribution of lateral sponsons.

as well as in the Phoenician, Greek, and Roman periods and down to about A.D. 1200, when they rather suddenly were replaced by stern rudders (Anderson, 1963, p. 86). We know almost nothing of early Arabic rudders except for the existence of a stern rudder in the thirteenth century (Casson, 1964, fig. 185). The distribution we see on Fig. 48 may well be relict from a former, much larger area. The possible significance of the Sri Lanka and Micronesia occurrences on shunting single outriggers has been discussed above; an earlier distribution of shunting may have had somewhat the same pattern as the map of the quarter rudder.

Sponsons, often in the form of fascines of bamboos lashed to both sides of narrow boats to provide stability and flotation, are common in mainland Southeast Asia but much less so farther eastward in the Pacific (Fig. 49). If Hornell's hypothesis is correct that these devices led eventually to the creation of double-outrigger canoes (1946, p. 267), then the place of origin for the double outrigger is most likely the Vietnamese coast, where contact with single outriggers and greater wave size than that found on inland rivers may have suggested spreading of the fascines outward from the gunwales on cross-beams.

When the maps for twelve of the most important Austronesian boat traits are analyzed (Figs. 37, 39–49), it then becomes possible to summarize them in a map of complexity of traits (Fig. 50). Arbitrary areas, usually island groups from New Guinea eastward but more selective in Indonesia,

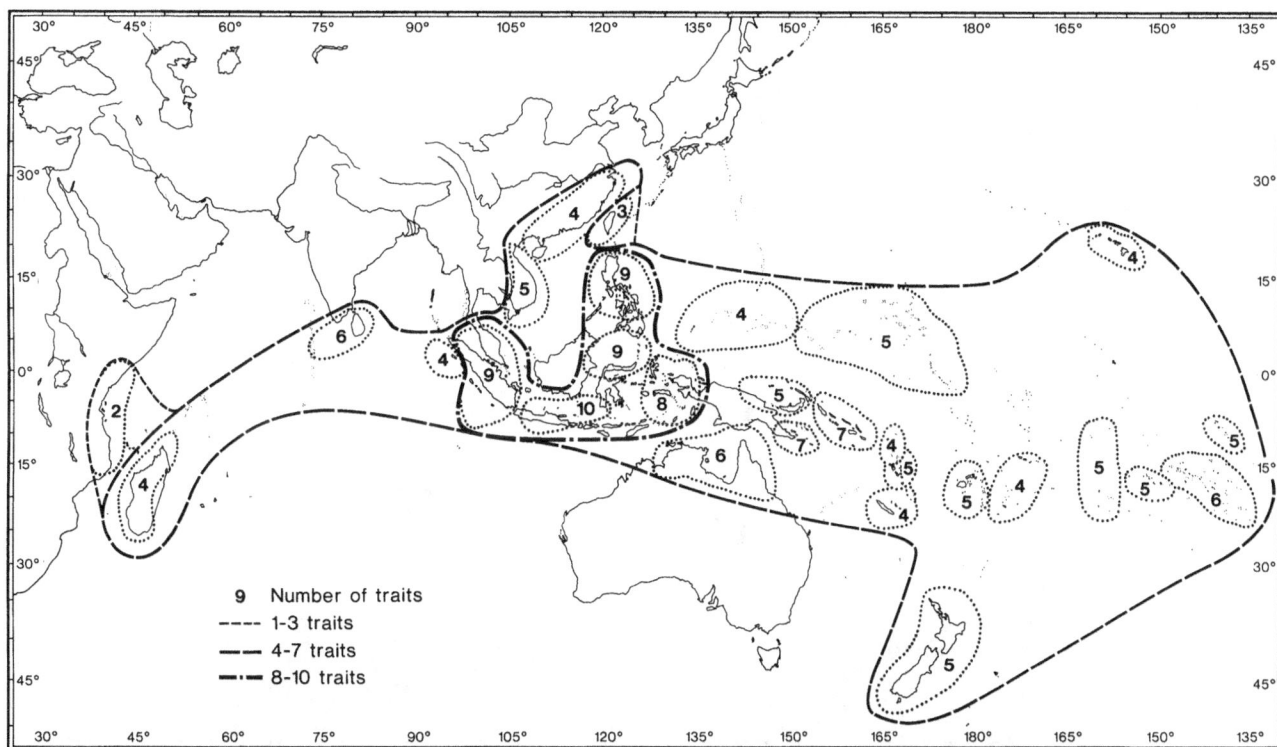

FIG. 50. Watercraft complexity based on twelve Austronesian boat traits.

can be established and the number of traits for each area counted. Centered on Sulawesi but including most of Indonesia is an area in which some eight to ten of the total of twelve traits are found. A much larger area extending from Madagascar to the Tuamotus has four to six traits. The extreme edges of the Austronesian area, Taiwan and the African coast, are the simplest, with one to three traits. If we hypothesize that a center of complexity is likely to have been a center of innovation from which traits flowed outward (a common hypothesis in plant geography, anthropology, and cultural geography) then central Indonesia is clearly the center of innovation for Austronesian boat traits.

In concluding our examination of distribu-

tional evidence, two traits which pertain to shunting and which may be of assistance in working out its history are presented. As we already have seen (Fig. 41), shunting is a universal trait in Micronesia and Melanesia, with curious extensions eastward into Polynesia and westward to Sri Lanka and Madagascar. The last two cases, plus the relict examples of single outriggers in Indonesia, make us suspect that the trait once extended across Indonesia and moved both eastward and westward. A logical extension of the idea of shunting is construction of canoes in which both ends are identical, having end symmetry as described earlier. Fig. 51 indicates the distribution of end symmetry as being conterminous from the Gilbert Islands west through Micronesia,

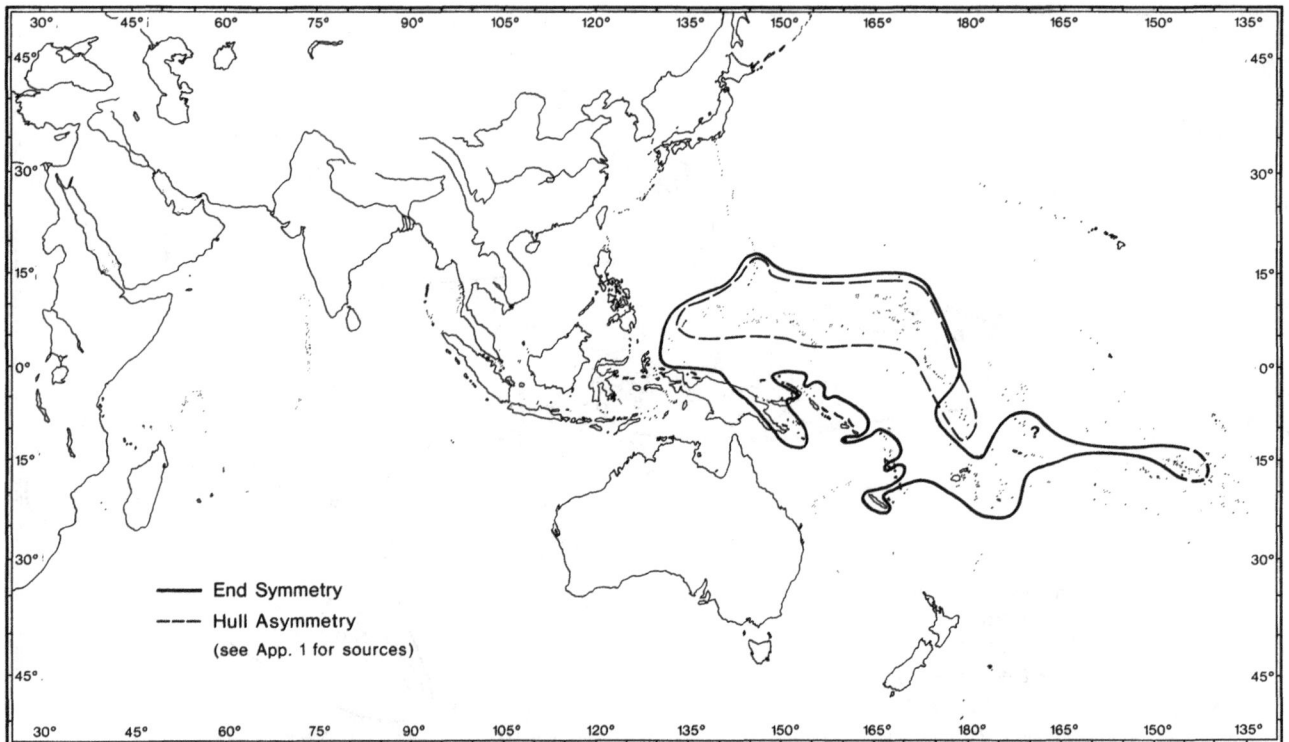

FIG. 51. Distribution of end symmetry and hull asymmetry.

south to New Guinea (Mapia Islands), and thence east to the Bismarcks, New Britain, and Rossel Island. A spotty alternation of end symmetry and its absence extends from Emirau and New Ireland through the Solomons and New Hebrides to New Caledonia. Fiji, Tonga, and Samoa have end-symmetrical canoes, and the far eastern extension is in the double canoes of the western Tuamotus. Contacts between Micronesia and Melanesia are well known, and the trait could have developed in either area, although Micronesia is probably the better bet (see below). How the trait reached Fiji is a puzzle, but its absence in the Ellice Islands leads one to suspect contacts from the New Hebrides or from the Santa Cruz Islands. (Linguistic relationships suggest the same conclusion [Pawley and Green, 1975, p. 26].)

The remaining trait, hull asymmetry, in which the outrigger side of the hull is more rounded than the flatter off side, is a sophisticated design feature that tends to counteract the couple caused by outrigger drag. It is solidly Micronesian in distribution, except for Palau and with the addition of the Ellice Islands, and leads to the hypothesis that maximum development of potential for shunting took place in that area (Fig. 51).

We infer, then, that shunting diffused eastward from Indonesia to a wide area. Endsymmetrical canoes may have originated in Micronesia, but the maximum development of shunting as a technique, the development of hull asymmetry, was indigenous to Micronesia, with the center of innovation somewhere in the Carolines, Marianas, or Marshall Islands.

7

Ages and Origins

〜〜〜〜〜〜〜〜〜〜〜〜〜〜〜〜〜〜〜〜〜〜〜〜〜〜〜〜〜〜〜〜〜〜〜〜〜〜

As we have seen above, the evidence of ethnology, physical anthropology, linguistics, and archaeology has converged so nicely in Polynesia that little argument remains about the area's culture history. During the first millennium B.C., pre-Polynesians in Tonga and Samoa developed full Polynesian culture and then spread in the first millennium A.D. over the remainder of Polynesia. To the west, in Micronesia and particularly in Melanesia, evidence from the several fields does not agree except in the general sense of origins still farther westward in Indonesia. Under these circumstances, and basing our hypotheses on the evidence of the last two chapters, we can make some reasonably positive assertions about Polynesia and some reasonable guesses for areas farther west. The watercraft evidence by itself, however, permits only a reasoned hypothesis about relative chronology and almost nothing in the way of absolute dating.

Little can be added to what has been said already about the more primitive types of watercraft in the Pacific. Most persons would agree with the reasoned inference that simplicity of construction makes it highly likely that bark boats and wood or bamboo rafts are the oldest types of watercraft in the Pacific. Rafts, as the simplest of devices floating by means of their own buoyancy,

are usually thought to be older than bark boats, which are displacement craft. But the distributional evidence from Australia, bark boats much farther to the south and east and with wider area (Fig. 36), suggests their greater antiquity and possible association with the thirty-thousand- to forty-thousand-year antiquity of man on that continent. The probably ancient but clearly unseaworthy bark rafts of the Tasmanians may be a retrogression from bark boats.

Dugout canoes, again, are usually thought to be of considerable antiquity but less ancient than rafts or bark boats because of the much greater effort required in dugout construction. The very wide distribution of dugouts suggests their antiquity and their probable replacement of rafts or bark boats in many places. In the Pacific they certainly antedate any multihulled craft but probably extended no farther eastward than the range shown in Fig. 39 because of obvious lack of seaworthiness on open waters. With the addition of stabilizing devices, doubling of canoes or addition of outriggers, they then became the vehicle of Pacific colonization.

As the study of hull and sail types in the previous chapter has indicated, it is highly probable that the oldest types of Austronesian multihulled craft are double canoes and tacking single-outrigger canoes. The distribution of these craft, far to the east in Polynesia but with relicts westward marking the trail along which migration took place (probably through Melanesia), is strongly suggestive (Figs. 40 and 41). Double canoes are probably somewhat older, because the relict trail leads all the way back to the Asiatic mainland, whereas no single-outrigger relicts (except for relatively recent examples in India and Madagascar) are to be found beyond Indonesia. The map of complexity of boat traits (Fig. 50) suggests that the single-outrigger modification probably took place in central Indonesia, centered on Sulawesi. The analysis of seaworthiness leads to the same conclusion about age, the outermost double canoes and tacking single outriggers being somewhat less seaworthy than later types to their west.

Reasonable inference from our rapidly developing knowledge of archaeology also leads to the same result. Polynesian ancestry back to the users of Lapita pottery in Tonga-Samoa about 1300 B.C. is unbroken, and it seems probable that the Lapita people were proto-Mongoloid, as are their present-day Polynesian descendants (Bellwood, 1979, pp. 244, 255). An equally probable inference is that the Lapita people used double canoes and tacking single outriggers in their very rapid movement eastward from New Guinea to the western edge of Polynesia.

The linguistic evidence also concurs. Pre-Polynesian languages had developed in Fiji-Tonga-Samoa by about 1000 B.C., and a reconstruction of proto-Polynesian indicates the use of multihulled craft (Pawley and Green, 1975, pp. 34, 42). Unfortunately, reconstructions of the words *katea* and *hama* for main hull and outrigger float or port hull (a usage continued to the present all over Polynesia) do not permit specific distinction of double canoe and single outrigger or any direct inference on tacking technique. From the other evidence above, however, it seems highly probable that both double canoes and tacking single outriggers were in use. The reconstruction of proto-Austronesian, at a time range of 3000–5000 B.C. somewhere in the Taiwan-Moluccas-Bismarcks area (Bellwood, 1979, p. 122), does permit a strong inference on the use of multihulled craft (Pawley and Green, 1975, p. 34) but again is not specific on type. It is a reasonable inference that the earlier craft were double canoes and that tacking single outriggers came into being in central Indonesia at about the same time that proto-Austronesian developed.

The evidence for age and origins of shunting single outriggers (and, rarely, shunting double canoes) is better in some ways, but less good in others, than that for double canoes and tacking single outriggers. Almost no trait found in archaeological sites can be tied, even inferentially, to shunting canoes as Lapita pottery can be tied, albeit loosely, to double canoes. Similarly, the evidence of linguistics presently available tells us nothing directly about shunting and very little inferentially. The best evidence is that of seaworthiness, which suggests intermediate age for shunting canoes, and distributions, which imply the same. Fortunately we have unequivocal evidence that shunting replaced tacking in Tonga between 1600 and 1800 and is unquestionably, therefore, the younger technique. The tongue of primitive crane spritsails and of shunting which leads eastward to the Tuamotus implies earlier diffusion eastward of the shunting trait in less sophisticated form, penetrating to the heart of the area of double canoes and tacking single outriggers in the first millennium A.D.

We have seen that the highest development of shunting canoes took place in Micronesia, the only area with both end symmetry and hull asymmetry. This observation might lead us logically to infer that this center of complexity was the place of origin of shunting until we note the disjunct distribution in Sri Lanka and Madagascar. The trait at one time must have extended across the width of Indonesia and diffused both eastward and westward, probably from the Indonesian center of boat complexity. A poor date of the first century A.D. (but better than none) for the westward movement comes from Pliny's garbled account of boats in Sri Lanka that have two bows and can move equally well with each (Plinius, 1855, book 6, chap. 24). If shunting canoes had reached Sri Lanka somewhat before the first century A.D., they must have existed in Indonesia a bit earlier still. A date for the invention of perhaps 1000 to 500 B.C., in the vicinity of Sulawesi, is a reasonable hypothesis at this stage of our knowledge.

It has been noted above that tacking double canoes have good stability and sail balance on both tacks, whereas tacking single outriggers have poor stability and worse sail balance when the float is to leeward. From this understanding we can assume that shunting was invented to rectify the poor aspects of tacking single outriggers, that sailors were probably reluctant to give up the known good qualities of tacking double canoes, and hence that shunting double canoes are a somewhat later development than shunting single outriggers. The latter, in fact, were so far superior that only in areas of recent changeover

(Samoa, Tonga, Fiji, New Caledonia, and possibly Mailu) did double canoes continue in use. Everywhere else in Micronesia and Melanesia they quickly vanished in the face of the new technology.

On the basis of the rather slender evidence of Fig. 51, I hypothesize that shunting in its early form (canoes without end symmetry) first spread eastward in both Melanesia and Micronesia, soon to be followed in both culture areas by more sophisticated canoes in which end symmetry bears witness to full acceptance of the new idea that both ends of the canoe are of equal importance as alternate bows. The later idea had spotty acceptance and rejection from the Solomon Islands eastward but did reach as far as Samoa and the Tuamotus. Finally, Micronesian genius in developing the idea to its utmost potential by developing the idea of hull asymmetry must be recognized.

Three sets of data may be tentatively hypothesized as related to shunting canoes. 1. The similar fishhooks of Micronesia, the Ellice Islands, the Tokelaus, and eastern Polynesia, bypassing western Polynesia (Bellwood, 1979, p. 320), may be related to a spread of primitive shunting into Polynesia, followed at a later date by the known thrust of shunting into Tonga and Samoa. 2. The appearance of an incised ware tradition in Fiji about A.D. 1000, together with the appearance and rapid development of fortifications, is thought to represent in-migration of a new group (Frost, 1979, p. 79). Another introduction of the new migrants may well have been the technique of shunting. The utility of fast shunting canoes in what seems to have been an increase in warfare would have been great, and the date is reasonable. 3. Again, the pottery lamps and infant burials in two jars occurring in Yap (Bellwood, 1979, p. 285) may be related to a relatively late introduction (A.D. 1000?) of quarter rudders from Indonesia into Micronesia.

Finally, let us consider what seems to be the youngest boat type in Austronesia, the double-outrigger canoe with boom lugsail. Relatively youthful age is clearly suggested by the analysis of seaworthiness and by its relatively central and small distribution compared to those of other boat and sail types. The Boro Bodur sculptures (about A.D. 800) give us a date which must be a long time after the beginning of the trait because of the high development of the seven different ships and because religious sculptures of traits almost certainly follow by some appreciable time the traits' inventions. A better clue on age comes from the disjunct distributions shown in Fig. 42—occurrences of double outriggers in Nissan and the Louisiades. These occurrences, the *mon* outriggerless plank boat of the Solomons, which is much like the *orembai* of the Moluccas, the double-outrigger canoes of Torres Strait and the Cape York Peninsula (Davidson, 1935, p. 73), and known trading activities east of Geelvink Bay (Forrest, 1780, p. 112) all indicate Indonesian activities well eastward of island Indonesia itself. When joined with the archaeological evidence of pottery similar to the Novaliches (Philippines) type in Collingwood Bay (eastern New Guinea), locations of jar burials, linguistic evidence, and distribution of Dongson art influences along the north coast of New Guinea and east to the Trobriand Islands, the sum strongly suggests Indonesian traders were in this area perhaps by

A.D. 500 (Bellwood, 1979, pp. 267, 269).

The suggested relationship with the Dongson culture of northern Vietnam, which extends from about 500 B.C. to about A.D. 100 (Bellwood, 1979, p. 185), gives a possible age clue for the onset and origin of double-outrigger canoes which may be helpful. Bellwood's map of the distribution of Dongson drums (1979, p. 188) coincides closely with that of boom lugsails and suggests a movement southward and eastward of double-outrigger canoes from an Annamese center of innovation. Hornell's hypothesis that double outriggers were derived from sponsons along the sides of river canoes may well have considerable validity when added to the idea that this innovation moved into a coastal area in which single outriggers were already in use. Outriggers are said to have been used in Vietnam formerly (Advanced Research Projects Agency, 1962, p. A-I-5, but with no source cited), and merit is added to the idea by the observation that some Vietnamese boats are very narrow and that the only Chinese junks which use balance boards are found nearby in Pakhoi (Audemard, 1957–1971, v. 8, p. 67). The changeover from single outriggers that shunt to double outriggers that tack can be explained tentatively by the equal speed but observed slower rate of capsize of the latter and, even more tentatively, by possible introduction of a new sail type, the boom lug, which lends itself far better to tacking than to shunting. We are on very weak ground here, of course, but the place and approximate time of the double-outrigger innovation, Vietnam in the early Christian era, are a bit more secure.

I hypothesize, then, that the multihulled

craft so typical of the Austronesians and the canoes which made their voyaging possible began with double canoes and were quickly followed by tacking single outriggers. Shunting single outriggers appeared later and were ultimately followed by double-outrigger canoes. Our consideration of Austronesian canoe ages and origins must conclude at this point, at exactly the place where it intersects with a still larger question of the ages and origins of sails and boats in general and with the possibility of connection between Southeast Asia and the worlds of China northward and India and Europe westward. Whether quarter rudders, boom lugsails, and spritsails are related to contacts in those directions is another book-length study which cannot be pursued here.

It is easy, from the present vantage point, to look backward and see where Haddon and Hornell went astray in their theoretical conclusions. They made allegations about seaworthiness based on inference but not on rigorous tests. They disregarded the evidence of the distributions which they themselves so painstakingly made it possible to map, particularly in overlooking the implications of the alluring trails of relicts which lead back to the west. They recognized the proper relative ages of sails but ignored the hull configurations associated with them. They completely neglected shunting as a trait which might be useful and instead concentrated on outrigger connectives, a complex set of traits which still has not been unravelled logically (I tried but could make no sense of connectives and abandoned them as useful clues). In short, the influence of the then popular migration wave theory was allowed to override their own hard-won evidence.

Future developments in linguistics and particularly in nautical and land archaeology, with their possibilities for recovery of hulls and other rig parts made from organic materials, may well invalidate some parts of the hypotheses advanced here. But the strong hypothesis on relative seaworthiness must be shown to be invalid by rigorous field tests, and the trait distributions must be satisfactorily accounted for in any new hypotheses which may be developed.

In the light of present-day knowledge, both Haddon and Hornell might well now agree that double outriggers are younger than double canoes and single outriggers. Of one thing we can be certain: without their monumental substantive contributions of fact in the earlier decades of this century, this book could not have been written.

For a final word I return to where I began—a world of coconut palms, snow-white beaches, and pellucid water with canoes gliding over its surface. Except for modern analogues such as the *Hokule'a* in its dramatic voyage to Tahiti and the Mailu *orou* canoes, which provide the only transportation for visiting anthropologists to their off-shore island, the double canoes have vanished. But single-outrigger canoes still tack at high speed across the lagoon at Raiatea, occasionally on fishing expeditions but more often with excited tourists aboard, and the single outriggers of Puluwat—*Mikael, Epifano, Maitong,* and *Moromelil*—shunt from side to side as they beat up to Truk for cigarettes and a visit with relatives. Mr. Nardi's double-outrigger *vinta* still fishes in Sulu, over the two hundred miles from Bongao to Zamboanga, sailing out in the early hours of the morning and back at noon to sell the catch and then nod at anchor while crewman Cousin Abdul nods in turn under the afternoon sun. The great days of exploration across the ocean and of raiding expeditions to far islands have vanished, but outrigger canoes in their thousands still sail the Austronesian seas.

APPENDIX 1

Sources for Distribution Maps

FIG. 37. *Rafts of Wood or Bamboo.*

Audemard, 1957–1971, v. 9, pp. 82, near Amoy; 83, Ningpo.

Audemard, 1957–1971, v. 10, p. 52, Luang Prabang to Vientiane.

Bowen, 1952, p. 188, Oman, Massawa, Yemen.

Bowen, 1956, p. 289, Punt.

Forrest, 1780, p. 263, Magindanao.

Great Britain, Admiralty, 1944*b*, pp. 58, common in Java; 59, Batavia.

Haddon, 1937, pp. 13, Loyalties; 24, Malekula; 114, Bougaineville; 120, Nissan; 135, New Ireland; 217, SE Papua; 241, Massim; 288, NE Papua.

Hornell, 1936, pp. 48, Marquesas; 93, Mangareva; 143, Societies; 217, New Zealand; 219, Chathams; 274, Tonga; 330, Fiji; 355, Gilberts; 412, Yap; 435, Palau.

Hornell, 1946, pp. 61, Adam's Bridge, Orissa, Cape Comorin, N of Ceylon, Colombo; 67, Laccadives; 68, Ganges lowlands, Assam; 69, Godaveri R.; 70, Queensland, Sulu, Manila, Wellesley I., ninety-mile beach to Bathurst I., two hundred mi. SW of King Sound, Shark Bay; 73, Bismarcks; 75, San Cristobal, Santa Cruz; 76, Torres Is.; 85, Lobito Bay.

Ling, 1956, p. 27, Formosa.

Mitman, 1923, p. 262, Malacca.

Nishimura, 1925, pp. 26, Japan; 62, Korea.

Paris, 1955, map 1, Vietnam.

Worcester, 1971, pp. 311, Anhwei; 418, Tungting Lake; 443, Miao-Hungkiang; 545, upper Yangtze; 587, Minkiang.

FIG. 39. *Simple Dugouts Without Outrigger.*

Audemard, 1957–1971, v. 10, p. 54, Vientiane.

Davidson, 1935, p. 73, N Australia.

Doran, 1970, field notes, Sulu.

Great Britain, Admiralty, 1944*b*, pp. 16, Palembang; 21, Lake Toba; 26, Sumatra river craft; 61, 80, Celebes rivers and creeks; 85, Buru; 121, Borneo rivers and creeks; 168, Malaita, Guadalcanal.

Greenhill, 1971, pp. 110, East Pakistan; 154, Calicut dugouts in Karachi, Persian Gulf, East Africa.

Greenhill, 1976, p. 139, Japan.

Haddon, 1920, p. 78, Andamans, Nicobars.

Haddon, 1937, pp. 99, Guadalcanal; 136, Tabar; 165, Admiralties; 205, Bamu R.; 210, Purari R.; 147, Milne Bay; 284, W of Cape Nelson; 293, Sialum; 294, Astrolabe Bay; 298, Sepik R.; 303, Aitape; 307, Malol-Nori; 310, Humboldt Bay; 331, Fakfak to Torres Strait. Negative: New Caledonia, New Hebrides, Polynesian outliers, San Cristobal, Nissan, most of New Ireland, Emirau, Mussau, New Britain, Massim.

Hornell, 1920*c*, pp. 68, Buru; 92, many on W coast of Borneo.

Hornell, 1923, pp. 144, Indus Delta, Hab R. (Baluchistan); 149, Ratnagiri, S of Goa; 161, Kilakarai; 176, Godaveri R.; 190, all over Burma, Inle Lake.

Hornell, 1936, pp. 200, New Zealand: Taranaki, Tolaga, Auckland, Tasman Bay, Otago?; 283, Uvea, Futuna. Negative: Hawaii, Marquesas, Tuamotus, Easter, Societies, Australs, Cooks, Samoa, Tokelaus, Tonga, Niue, Rotuma, Ellices, Gilberts, Marshalls, Carolines, Palau.

Hornell, 1946, p. 186, N Australia.

Ling, 1970, p. 72, Hunan, Kwangsi, Taiwan.

Needham, 1971, pp. 388, Szechwan, Changchow; 392, Yellow R.; 396, Yalu R.

Neyret, 1970, p. 3, Manila.

Nooteboom, 1932, pp. 21, Palembang; 53, Engano; 64, Mentawei; 81, SE Borneo; 144, Java; 164, Bali; 184, Halmahera; 200, Lombok, S New Guinea.

Smyth, 1929, pp. 381, Mergui; 401, Malaysia; 402, Siam, Burma.

Sopher, 1957, pp. 18, Malabar coast; 19, Orissa coast.

Sopher, 1958, pp. 6, N Ceylon, Puttalam Lagoon; 12, Bengal; 13, Cox's Bazaar.

Sopher, 1959, pp. 21, Goa; 27, Malabar; 28, Malabar canoes in Gujerat; 33, Diu.

Television program *Views of Asia*, 1979, Malaya, Sabah.

FIG. 40. *Double Canoes*.

Audemard, 1957–1971, v. 10, p. 53, upper Mekong.

Doran, 1977, photograph, Java.

Forrest, 1780, p. 230, Mindanao.

Great Britain, Admiralty, 1944*b*, p. 82, Palopo (Celebes) (3 hulls).

Haddon, 1920, p. 77, Nanusa, Malabar, Ganges.

Haddon, 1937, pp. 35, Pentecost; 40, Ontong Java?, Taumako; 98, Malaita?; 179, Aua (W of Ninigo); 202–237, Fly R. to Samarai (3 or 2 hulls); 264, Rossel I.; 328, Geelvink Bay (4 hulls).

Hornell, 1923, p. 176, Coromandel.

Hornell, 1936, p. 443, Truk, all of Polynesia.

Hornell, 1946, p. 248, Benares.

Hornell, 1950, p. 105, Cochin.

Ling, 1970, p. 165, NE China.

Needham, 1971, p. 392, Grand Canal, Ichang.

Nooteboom, 1932, p. 112, Celebes (4 hulls); 144, East Java.

Smyth, 1895, p. 48, upper Mekong R.

Suder, 1930, pp. 73–76, Ganges, Tsang-po, Tarim, Mesopotamia, Lake Victoria.

Worcester, 1971, pp. 462, Ichang, Wei R.; 150, 285, 419, 458, Yangtze R.

FIG. 41. *Single-Outrigger Canoes*.

Great Britain, Admiralty, 1944*b*, pp. 28, N Java; 60, Makassar; 61, Celebes rivers and harbors; 74, S Celebes; 107, Kei Is.; 124, N Borneo.

Haddon, 1920, pp. 78, Andamans, Nicobars, Sumatra, Mentawei, Sarawak (toy), Sangir, Ceylon, S India, Goa, Cochin, Maldives; 79, Geelvink Bay and eastward.

Hornell, 1920*c*, pp. 77, Manila; 80, S Celebes (not in N); 89, Makassar; 104, Mentawei; 105, S India, Ceylon.

Hornell, 1923, pp. 178, Cuddalore (India); 227, whole distribution.

Hornell, 1934, p. 40, Comoro Is.

Hornell, 1946, p. xxiv, whole distribution.

Mowll, 1980, letters, Batangas, Tayabas Bay (Philippines).

Nooteboom, 1932, p. 220, Kei, Babar, Makassar, N Java.

Sopher, 1958, p. 5, S and E of Ceylon.

Sopher, 1959, pp. 28, Daman; 36, fifty mi. NW of Karachi.

FIG. 43. *Double Spritsail*.

Bowen, 1959, p. 158, map.

Hornell, 1920*b*, p. 139, W coast of Madagascar.

Hornell, 1934, p. 319, "Sumatra."

Hornell, 1943, p. 41, SW Ceylon.

Paris, 1841–1843, plate 2, "Moka" (Yemen).

Villiers, 1957, p. 846, Maldive Is. (I thank Mrs. Evelyn King for locating this source.)

FIG. 44. *Oceanic Spritsail*.

Doran, 1970, field notes, Bongao, Jolo (Sulu).

Haddon, 1937, pp. 25–39, N New Hebrides and Banks; 199, Mawata (New Guinea).

Hornell, 1936, pp. 147, Australs?; 171, Atiu?; 495, basic map for Polynesia; 400, Ponape.

Nooteboom, 1932, pp. 128, Makassar; 145, 149, East Java.

Wernstedt and Spencer, 1967, p. 364, Panay (Philippines).

FIG. 45. *Crane Spritsail and Primitive Crane Spritsail.*

Distribution of crane spritsails about 1850.

Forrest, 1780, p. 89, Asia Is.

Haddon, 1937, pp. 9, New Caledonia; 16, Tanna (New Hebrides); 20, Efate; 25, 29, 39, definitely absent in N New Hebrides; 49, Santa Cruz; 62, Rennell; 72, Ontong Java?; 77, Taku; 78, Nuguria?; 268, Trobriands; 273, D'Entrecasteaux.

Hornell, 1936, pp. 167, Aitutaki?; 445, Micronesia, Ellice, Fiji, Tonga, Samoa.

Lessa, 1978, p. 244, Mapia Is.

Distribution of primitive crane spritsails about 1850.

Haddon, 1937, pp. 213, Orokolo (Gulf of Papua); 228, Cape Possession to Cape Rodney (centered on Port Moresby); 236, Mailu.

Hornell, 1920*c*., pp. 96–100, Bali, Madura, East Java ("Madura lateen").

Hornell, 1936, p. 445, Manihiki, Tuamotus.

Known change from primitive crane sprit to crane sprit, about 1750–1850.

Hornell, 1936, pp. 241, Samoa; 248, Tokelau?; 272, Tonga; 282, Rotuma?; 283, Uvea; 288, Niutoputapu; 303, Ellice?.

FIG. 46. *Boom Lugsails.*

Trapezial boom lug.

Paris, 1955, Carte 1, N limit at Thanh Hoa (Vietnam).

Remote Area Conflict Information Center, 1967*a*, pp. 241, 301, Saigon to Quang Tri; 359, An Xuyen to Quang Tri; 393, Saigon to Quang Tri.

Remote Area Conflict Information Center, 1967*b*, p. 363, Phrachuap Khiri Khan to Trat (Thailand).

Smyth, 1929, p. 436, Cambodian coast.

Square boom lug.

Atkinson, 1905, p. 163, "Philippines."

Folkard, 1870, p. 267, Achen (Sumatra).

Great Britain, Admiralty, 1944*b*, pp. 15, N coast of Sumatra, 18, S and SW coasts of Sumatra; 22, N, E, and SE coasts of Sumatra; 123, Brunei (Borneo).

Remote Area Conflict Information Center, 1967*b*, pp. 259, entire Thailand coast on Gulf of Siam, W coast at Ranong; 391, Gulf of Siam near Malaysia.

Paris, 1841–1843, plate 74, Manila.

Smyth, 1929, pp. 379, Mergui Arch.; 392, W coast of Thailand; 394, Singora (Songkhla, Thailand); 406, Selangor (near Kuala Lumpur); 411, Malacca; 417, Menam R.

Rectangular boom lug.

Casson, 1964, pp. 174, Java; 175, Celebes; 203, Malaya; 205, Java.

Doran, 1970, field notes, all of Sulu Arch.

Folkard, 1870, pp. 256, Moluccas; 257, near Makassar; 260, Amboina, Batjan; 266, Sumatra.

Great Britain, Admiralty, 1944*b*, pp. 24, Banka; 25, Billiton; 28, all Java; 55, Bali, 71, S Celebes; 72, Gulf of Tomini; 76, N Celebes; 78, W Celebes; 80, Gulf of Mandar (Celebes); 85, Buru; 88, Ternate, Kei; 90, all Halmahera; 105, Flores; 116, Lombok, Sumbawa; 118, Wetar, N Timor.

Hornell, 1920*c*, pp. 51, Geelvink Bay; 56, Waigeo; 60, Galela (Halmahera); 71, Buru; 85, Menado (Celebes); 86, NW Celebes; 88, Makassar; 92, W Borneo; 101, all Celebes, N Java; 102, Bali.

Hornell, 1946, p. 205, between second and fourth cataracts on the Nile.

Mowll, 1980, letter, Cagayan (Mindanao).

Nooteboom, 1932, pp. 97, Talaud; 113, Menado, Makassar; 172, East Java; 184, Halmahera; 193, Wetar.

Paris, 1882–1908, plate 64, Bayonne (France); plate 324, Gorée (Senegal).

Pritchett, 1899, p. 135, Persian Gulf.

Wallace, 1869, p. 367, Ceram.

Primitive rectangular lug.

Haddon, 1937, pp. 152, Vitu Is., Talasea Penin. and W; 154, W end of New Britain; 158, Siassi; 162, Arawe (New Britain); 165, 169, Admiralties; 170, Kaniet; 174, Hermits; 176, Ninigo; 196, Torres Strait; 199, Mawata coast (New Guinea); 201, Fly R. estuary; 241, Fyfe Bay (E tip of New Guinea); 244, E of Fyfe Bay; 246, Daui; 249, Samarai; 252, Tubetube Is.; 253, Wari; 255, Calvados; 258, Tagula; 261, Rossel; 265, Murua I. (trade canoes to Wari); 289, Huon Penin.; 290, Tami Is.; 292, Finsch Harbor; 297, Astrolabe Bay; 299, LeMaire (Schouten Is.); 305, Aitape; 308, Vanimo; 313,

Humboldt Bay (Hollandia); 316, Wakde (same as
Humboldt Bay).

FIG. 47. *Common Spritsail.*

With boom.
Atkinson, 1905, p. 41, Pasig R. (Luzon).
Doran, 1970, field notes, Jolo, Bongao (Sulu).
Great Britain, Admiralty, 1944b, pp. 76, N Celebes;
    85, Buru?; 105, Flores; 114, Sumba, Sumbawa;
    124, Sarawak?.
Haddon, 1937, pp. 21, Efate; 67, Sikaiana?; 113,
    Shortlands?.
Hornell, 1920c, pp. 71, Buru?; 86, NW Celebes; 96,
    Bali; 100, East Java?
Hornell, 1936, pp. 18, Hawaii [1839]; 74, Fakarava
    (Tuamotus); 125, Raiatea; 167, Cooks?.
Neyret, 1970, pp. 8, Las Palmas (Mindanao); 11,
    Zamboanga.
Paris, 1841–1843, plate 71, Manila Bay.
Smyth, 1929, pp. 408–409, Singapore.

Without boom.
Audemard, 1957–1971, v. 9, p. 48, Chusan Arch.; 50,
    Chusan to Amoy.
Casson, 1954, p. 218, Saloniki to Asia Minor (first to
    third centuries A.D.)
Casson, 1964, p. 153, Marseilles (about 1800).
Great Britain, Admiralty, 1944b, pp. 57, West Java;
    120, SE Borneo.
Haddon, 1937, p. 117, Nissan?.
Hornell, 1923, p. 177, Pulicat Lake (near Madras).
Hornell, 1946, p. 242, Ganges R.
Mitman, 1923, pp. 229, Lithuania; 234, Jutland; 242,
    Gotland; 244, Sciathos.
Moore, 1925, pp. 147, Thames R.; 157, Holland; 158,
    Orkneys; 160, Greek Is, Bosporus; 162, Malta;
    166, Bug R. (E of Odessa).
Needham, 1971, p. 393, Formosa?.
Neyret, 1970, pp. 3, Casiguran Bay (Luzon); 5, Jolo
    (Sulu).
Nooteboom, 1932, pp. 81, SE Borneo; 128, Makassar.
Paris, 1841–1843, plate 72, Manila.
Paris, 1882–1908, plate 59, Black Sea (Turkey); plate
    77, Constantinople; plate 82, Ligurian coast
    (Italy); plate 204, Sporades (Greece); plate 234,
    Dnieper R.

Phillips-Birt, 1962, pp. 76, NW Europe [earliest,
    1420]; 80, Dordrecht (Netherlands), Senegal,
    Bosporus, Gulf of Smyrna; fig. 44, Enkhuizen
    (Netherlands).
Smyth, 1929, pp. 36, Sjaelland (Denmark); 39, Born-
    holm; 41, N Jutland; 42, Sweden (W?); 55, Oslo;
    71, Holland; 121, Orkneys; 164, Thames R.; 198,
    Brighton; 202, Portsmouth; 234, Falmouth; 245,
    Mersey; 282, Lipari (Italy); 292, Naples; 321,
    Turkish coaster; 324, Smyrna; 325–327, Constan-
    tinople, Bosporus; 399, Singapore.
Worcester, 1971, pp. 180, Ningpo; 183, Chusan; 206,
    Shanghai to Hangchow; 211, 220, Shanghai; 267,
    Wusih; 268, Kiangsu near Shanghai; 418,
    Changsha.

FIG. 48. *Quarter Rudder.*

Doran, 1970, field notes, Sulu, Zamboanga.
Doran, 1975, p. 88, Yap to Puluwat.
Great Britain, Admiralty, 1944b, pp. 24, Bangka, Bil-
    liton; 32, Java; 34, 43, Madura; 44, East Java; 53,
    Bali; 63, Makassar; 72, Gulf of Tomini; 76, all of
    Celebes; 90, Halmahera; 98, Ambon; 114, Flores;
    116, Sumbawa; 119, Wetar; 120, Borneo; 124,
    Sarawak.
Hornell, 1920c, p. 70, Buru.
Hornell, 1923, pp. 158, W Ceylon; 169, Palk Strait;
    188, 189, Ganges R.; 190, Burma.
Neyret, 1970, pp. 6, Manila; 10, Sulu.
Nooteboom, 1932, pp. 64, Mentawei; 192, Tanimbar;
    200, Timor.
Paris, 1955, map 2, India to Indonesia.
Smyth, 1929, pp. 364, Ganges; 365, Bengal; 372, Irra-
    waddy R.; 379, Mergui; 400, Singora; 406, Se-
    langor; 413, Madura; 428, Gulf of Siam; 448,
    Menam R.

Negative evidence, critical locations.
Audemard, 1957–1971, v. 8, not in S China.
Haddon, 1937, pp. 49, not in Santa Cruz; 160, not in
    Siassi; 162, not in Arawe; 169, not in Bismarcks;
    175, not in Hermit Is.
Hornell, 1920b, p. 137, not in Madagascar.
Hornell, 1923, pp. 140–150, not in W India.
Hornell, 1936, pp. 349, not in Gilberts; 370, not in
    Marshalls; 386, Sonsorol?; 399, "Mokil like Mar-

shalls"; 415, Marianas used paddle; 433, Palau used steering oar.

FIG. 49. *Sponsons on Sides of Canoes.*

Audemard, 1957–1971, v. 10, plate 25, central Vietnam coast; plate 41, Vientiane; plate 42, Luang Prabang.

Greenhill, 1971, p. 105, Bengal.

Haddon, 1937, p. 110, Shortland Is.

Haddon and Hornell, 1938, p. 21, Shweli R., N Shan states.

Hornell, 1936, p. 30, Marquesas, Burma, Siam, Philippines, Solomons.

Neyret, 1970, p. 8, Moluccas, Manila.

Smyth, 1895, p. 47, Mekong near Luang Prabang.

Smyth, 1929, p. 364, Mekong; 396, E coast of Malaya.

Fig. 51. *End Symmetry and Hull Asymmetry.*

Hornell, 1936.

Page	Place	End Symmetry		Hull Asymmetry	
		Yes	No	Yes	No
85	Tuamotu	x			x
224	Samoa		x		
242	Samoa	x			
263	Tonga	x			
268	Tonga		x		
275	Niue		x		x
280	Rotuma	x	x		
283	Uvea	x			
286	Futuna		x		
292	Ellice		x		
297	Ellice			x	
311	Fiji	x			x
346	Gilbert	x		x	
362	Marshall	x		x	
375	Caroline	x		x	
381	Yap			x	
386	Yap	x			x
388	Tobi	x			x
389	Sonsorol	x			x
391	Mapia	x			x
397	Kapingamarangi		x		x

Page	Place	End Symmetry		Hull Asymmetry	
		Yes	No	Yes	No
414	Mariana	x		x	
425	Palau	x		x	x

Haddon, 1937.

Page	Place	End Symmetry		Hull Asymmetry	
		Yes	No	Yes	No
4	New Caledonia	x			x
13	Loyalty		x		
16	Tanna	x			x?
19	Aniwa				x
21	Efate		x		
23	Malekula	x			x
27	Malekula		x		x
28	Futuna		x		x?
32	Malekula	x			
36	Oba		x		x
36	Banks		x		x?
45, 48	Santa Cruz	x			x
55	Tikopia		x		x
58	Anuda		x		x
60	Rennell	x			x?
64	Bellona				x
65, 57	Sikaiana		x		x
70	Ontong Java		x		x?
76, 77	Taku	x	x		
79	Nuguria		x		
85	San Cristobal		x		x?
99	Guadalcanal		x		x
115	Buka		x?		x
117	Nissan				x
122	Tanga	x			x
128	Gazelle Peninsula	x	x		x
131	Watom		x		x
134	Lihir		x		x?
140	N New Ireland		x		x
143	Lavongai		x		x
146	Emirau		x		x
151	NW New Britain	x			x
158	Siassi	x			x
162	Arawe	x?			x
167	Admiralty	x?			x
170	Kaniet	x			x
172	Hermit	x			x
175	Ninigo	x			x

Page	Place	End Symmetry		Hull Asymmetry		Page	Place	End Symmetry		Hull Asymmetry	
		Yes	No	Yes	No			Yes	No	Yes	No
177	Aua	x			x?	284	S of Cape Nelson	x			x
206	Fly River		x		x	285	Orokaiva	x			x
212	Gulf of Papua		x		x	292	Finsch Harbor	x			x
221	Port Moresby		x		x	295, 297	Astrolabe Bay	x			x
234	Mailu	x			x	306	Tamara	x			x
244	W of Samarai	x			x	314	Humboldt Bay	x			x
245	Fyfe Bay	x			x	316	Arimoa		x		x
260	Rossel	x			x	318	Ansus		x		x
263	Louisiades	x			x	326	Geelvink Bay		x		x
272	D'Entrecasteaux	x			x						

Watercraft Complexity

Location	Ra	Dug	DC	OC	OCO	DS	OcS	CrS	BL	CoS	QR	Sp	Total
Swahili coast		x			x								2
Madagascar		x		x	x	x							4
Sri Lanka	x	x	x	x		x					x		6
Nias		x		x	x	x							4
Malaya-Sumatra	x	x	x	x	x				x	x	x	x	9
Java-Makassar	x	x	x	x	x		x	x	x	x	x		10
Moluccas–Geelvink Bay		x	x	x	x				x	x	x	x	8
Celebes Sea	x	x	x	x	x		x		x	x	x		9
Annam	x	x	x						x			x	5
S China	x	x	x							x			4
Formosa	x	x								x			3
N Philippines	x	x		x	x		x		x	x	x	x	9
W Micronesia	x			x				x			x		4
E Micronesia	x		x	x			x	x					5
Bismarcks	x	x	x	x					x				5
Massim	x	x	x	x	x			x	x				7
Solomons	x	x	x	x	x					x		x	7
N New Hebrides	x		x	x				x					4
Central New Hebrides	x		x	x			x			x			5
S New Hebrides– New Caledonia	x	x	x					x					4
Fiji	x	x	x	x				x					5
Tonga-Samoa	x		x	x				x					4

Location	Traits												
	Ra	Dug	DC	OC	OCO	DS	OcS	CrS	BL	CoS	QR	Sp	Total
Cooks			x	x			x	x		x			5
Societies	x		x	x			x			x			5
Tuamotus	x		x	x			x	x		x			6
Marquesas	x		x	x			x					x	5
Hawaii			x	x			x			x			4
New Zealand	x	x	x	x			x						5
N Australia	x	x		x	x		x		x				6

KEY:

Ra	Rafts		OcS	Oceanic spritsails
Dug	Dugouts without outriggers		CrS	Crane spritsails
DC	Double canoes		BL	Boom lugsails
OC	Single-outrigger canoes		CoS	Common spritsails
OCO	Double-outrigger canoes		QR	Quarter rudders
DS	Double spritsails		Sp	Sponsons

Bibliography

Advanced Research Projects Agency. 1962. *Junk Blue Book: A Handbook of Junks of South Vietnam.* Washington: Department of Defense.

Allen, Jim. 1979. Personal communication of October 24.

Amateur Yacht Research Society. 1972. Cover photograph and caption, *AYRS Airs*, No. 4 (November). Woodacres, Hythe, Kent: the society.

Anderson, Romola, and R. C. Anderson. 1926. *The Sailing Ship.* London: Harrap. Reprinted. New York: Norton, 1963.

Atkinson, Fred W. 1905. *The Philippine Islands.* New York: Ginn.

Audemard, Louis. 1957–1971. *Les Jonques Chinoises.* 10 vols. Rotterdam: Maritiem Museum Prins Hendrik.

Barbetti, M., and H. Allen. 1972. "Prehistoric Man at Lake Mungo, Australia, by 32,000 Years BP." *Nature* 240:46–48.

Bellwood, Peter. 1975. "The Prehistory of Oceania." *Current Anthropology* 16:9–17.

————. 1979. *Man's Conquest of the Pacific.* New York: Oxford University Press.

Birdsell, Joseph B. 1977. "The Recalibration of a Paradigm for the First Peopling of Greater Australia." In *Sunda and Sahul*, ed. J. Allen, J. Golson, and R. Jones, pp. 113–167. New York: Academic Press.

Boehmer, Richard. 1979. "Analysis of Sailing Vessel Performance Ratios and Their Synthesis." *AYRS Journal*, no. 93:31–41. Newbury, Berkshire: Amateur Yacht Research Society.

Bowen, Richard LeB., Jr. 1952. "Primitive Watercraft of Arabia." *American Neptune* 12:186–221.

————. 1953. "Eastern Sail Affinities." *American Neptune* 13:81–117, 185–211.

————. 1956. "Boats of the Indus Civilization." *Mariner's Mirror* 42:279–290.

————. 1959. "The Origins of Fore-and-Aft Rigs." *American Neptune* 19:155–199, 274–306.

Bruce, E., and H. A. Morss, Jr. 1976. *Design for Fast Sailing.* Newbury, Berkshire: Amateur Yacht Research Society.

Buck, Peter H. 1938. *Vikings of the Pacific.* Chicago: University of Chicago Press.

Casson, Lionel. 1954. "The Sails of the Ancient Mariner." *Archaeology* 7:214–219.

————. 1964. *Illustrated History of Ships and Boats.* Garden City, N.Y.: Doubleday.

————. 1971. *Ships and Seamanship in the Ancient World.* Princeton, N.J.: Princeton University Press.

Collins, G. E. P. 1937. *East Monsoon.* New York: Scribner's.

Davidson, D. S. 1935. "The Chronology of Australian Watercraft." *Journal of the Polynesian Society* 44:1–16, 69–84, 137–152, 193–207.

Dodd, Edward. 1972. *Polynesian Seafaring.* New York: Dodd, Mead.

Doran, Edwin, Jr. 1967. The Origin of Leeboards. *Mariner's Mirror* 53:39–53.

————. 1971. "The Sailing Raft as a Great Tradition." In *Man Across the Sea*, ed. C. Riley et al., pp. 115–136. Austin: University of Texas Press.

————. 1972. "Wa, Vinta, and Trimaran." *Journal of the Polynesian Society* 81:144–159.

————. 1974. "Outrigger Ages." *Journal of the Polynesian Society* 83:130–140.

———. 1975. "Puluwat Canoe Speeds." *Geoscience and Man* 12:83–89.

———. 1976. "Parallelism of Outrigger Floats." *AYRS Journal* 83B:18–22.

———. 1977. Photograph of double canoe model, Java. Leiden: Rijksmuseum voor Volkenkunde, catalog no. 37 M 588.

———. 1979. "Catamaran Stability—A Comment." *Multihulls* 5:63.

———. Forthcoming. "Five Outrigger Canoes of Sulu." In *The Fishing Culture of the World*, ed. Béla Gunda. Debrecen?: Hungarian Academic Press.

Emory, Kenneth P. 1979. "The Societies." In *The Prehistory of Polynesia*, ed. Jesse D. Jennings, pp. 200–221. Cambridge: Harvard University Press.

Finney, Ben R. 1967. "New Perspectives on Polynesian Voyaging." In *Polynesian Culture History*, ed. G. Highland et al., pp. 141–166. Honolulu: Bishop Museum Press.

———. 1977. "Voyaging Canoes and the Settlement of Polynesia." *Science* 196:1277–1285.

———. 1979a. *Hokule'a: The Way to Tahiti*. New York: Dodd, Mead.

———. 1979b. "Voyaging." In *The Prehistory of Polynesia*, ed. J. D. Jennings, pp. 323–351. Cambridge: Harvard University Press.

Folkard, H. C. 1870. *The Sailing Boat*. London: Longmans, Green. Reprinted. East Ardsley, Wakefield, Yorkshire: EP Publications, 1973.

Forrest, Thomas. 1780. *A Voyage to New Guinea and the Moluccas*. London: G. Scott. Reprinted. Kuala Lumpur: Oxford, 1969.

Frost, Everett L. 1979. "Fiji." In *The Prehistory of Polynesia*, ed. J. D. Jennings, pp. 61–81. Cambridge: Harvard University Press.

Gladwin, Thomas. 1970. *East is a Big Bird*. Cambridge: Harvard University Press.

Great Britain, Admiralty. 1944a. *Netherlands East Indies*. B.R. 518, Geographical Handbook Series. 2 vols. London: Naval Intelligence.

———. 1944b. *Fishing and Trading Craft of the Netherlands East Indies, New Guinea, and the Solomon Islands*. B.R. 1050C. London: Naval Intelligence.

Greenhill, Basil. 1971. *Boats and Boatmen of Pakistan*. Newton Abbot: David and Charles.

———. 1976. *Archaeology of the Boat*. Middletown, Conn.: Wesleyan University Press.

Green, Roger C. 1979. "Lapita." In *The Prehistory of Polynesia*, ed. J. D. Jennings, pp. 27–60. Cambridge: Harvard University Press.

Haddon, A. C. 1918. "The Outrigger Canoes of East Africa." *Man* 18:49–54.

———. 1920. "The Outriggers of Indonesian Canoes." *Journal of the Royal Anthropological Institute* 50:69–134.

———. 1937. *Canoes of Oceania*, vol. 2, *The Canoes of Melanesia, Queensland, and New Guinea*. B. P. Bishop Museum Special Publication 28. Reprinted (3 vols. in 1). Honolulu: Bishop Museum Press, 1975.

———, and James Hornell. 1938. *Canoes of Oceania*, vol. 3, *Definition of Terms, General Survey, and Conclusions*. B. P. Bishop Museum Special Publication 29. Reprinted (3 vols. in 1). Honolulu: Bishop Museum Press, 1975.

Hoerner, Sighard F. 1965. *Fluid-Dynamic Drag*. Published by the author.

Hornell, James. 1919. "The Affinities of East African Outrigger Canoes." *Man* 19:97–100.

———. 1920a. "Les pirogues à balancier de Madagascar et de l'Afrique orientale." *La Geographie* 34:1–23.

———. 1920b. "The Common Origin of the Outrigger Canoes of Madagascar and East Africa." *Man* 20:134–139.

———. 1920c. "The Outrigger Canoes of Indonesia." *Madras Fisheries Bulletin* 12:43–114.

———. 1923. "The Origins and Ethnological Significance of Indian Boat Designs." *Memoirs of the Asiatic Society of Bengal* 7:139–256.

———. 1934. "Indonesian Influence on East African Culture." *Journal of the Royal Anthropological Institute* 64:305–332.

———. 1936. *Canoes of Oceania*, vol. 1, *The Canoes of Polynesia, Fiji, and Micronesia*. B. P. Bishop Museum Special Publication 27. Reprinted (3 vols. in 1). Honolulu: Bishop Museum Press, 1975.

———. 1943. "The Fishing and Coastal Craft of Ceylon." *Mariner's Mirror* 29:40–53.

———. 1946. *Water Transport*. Cambridge: The University Press. Reprinted. Newton Abbot: David and Charles, 1970.

———. 1950. *Fishing in Many Waters*. Cambridge: The University Press.

Horridge, G. Adrian. 1978. *The Design of Planked Boats of the Moluccas*. Maritime Monographs and Reports, No. 38. Greenwich: National Maritime Museum.

———. 1979*a*. *The Lambo or Prahu Bot: A Western Ship in an Eastern Setting*. Maritime Monographs and Reports, No. 39. Greenwich: National Maritime Museum.

———. 1979*b*. *The Konjo Boatbuilders and the Bugis Prahus of South Sulawesi*. Maritime Monographs and Reports, No. 40. Greenwich: National Maritime Museum.

Horvath, S., and B. Finney. 1976. "Paddling Experiments and the Question of Polynesian Voyaging." In *Pacific Navigation and Voyaging*, ed. B. Finney, pp. 47–54. Wellington: The Polynesian Society.

Howard, Alan. 1967. "Polynesian Origins and Migrations." In *Polynesian Culture History*, ed. G. Highland et al., pp. 45–101. Honolulu: Bishop Museum Press.

Howells, William. 1973. *The Pacific Islanders*. New York: Scribner's.

———. 1977. "The Sources of Human Variation in Melanesia and Australia." In *Sunda and Sahul*, ed. J. Allen, J. Golson, and R. Jones, pp. 169–186. New York: Academic Press.

Jennings, Jesse D., ed. 1979. *The Prehistory of Polynesia*. Cambridge: Harvard University Press.

Johnson, Pamela. 1974. "Indonesian outrigger canoe." *New Pacific* 1, cover photo.

Johnstone, Paul. 1980. *The Sea-craft of Prehistory*. Cambridge: Harvard University Press.

Jones, Rhys. 1977. "Man as an Element of a Continental Fauna: The Case of the Sundering of the Bassian Bridge." In *Sunda and Sahul*, ed. J. Allen, J. Golson, and R. Jones, pp. 317–386. New York: Academic Press.

Jordan, Robert P. 1979. "Sri Lanka: Time of Testing." *National Geographic* 155:123–150.

Kroeber, Alfred L. 1948. *Anthropology*. New York: Harcourt, Brace.

Lauer, Peter K. 1970. "Sailing with the Amphlett Islanders." *Journal of the Polynesian Society* 79:381–398.

Lessa, William A. 1978. "The Mapia Islands and Their Affinities." In *The Changing Pacific*, ed. G. Gunson, pp. 228–246. New York: Oxford.

Levison, M., R. Ward, and J. Webb. 1973. *The Settlement of Polynesia: A Computer Simulation*. Minneapolis: University of Minnesota Press.

Lewis, David. 1972. *We, the Navigators*. Honolulu: University Press of Hawaii.

———. 1978. "The Pacific Navigators' Debt to the Ancient Seafarers of Asia." In *The Changing Pacific*, ed. G. Gunson, pp. 46–66. New York: Oxford.

Lewthwaite, Gordon R. 1967. "Geographical Knowledge of the Pacific Peoples." In *The Pacific Basin*, ed. H. R. Friis, pp. 57–86. New York: American Geographical Society.

Ling Shun-sheng. 1956. "Formosan Sea-going Raft and Its Origin in Ancient China." *Bulletin of the Institute of Ethnology, Academia Sinica* 1:1–54.

———. 1970. *A Study of the Raft, Outrigger, Double, and Deck Canoes of Ancient China, the Pacific, and the Indian Oceans*. Monograph No. 16. Taipei, Taiwan: Institute of Ethnology, Academia Sinica.

Marchaj, C. A. 1964. *Sailing Theory and Practice*. New York: Dodd, Mead.

———. 1979. *Aero-hydrodynamics of Sailing*. New York: Dodd, Mead.

Mitman, Carl W. 1923. *Catalogue of the Watercraft Collection in the United States National Museum*. Smithsonian Institution Bulletin No. 127. Washington: Government Printing Office.

Moore, Sir Alan. 1925. *Last Days of Mast and Sail*. Oxford: Clarendon Press. Reprinted. Newton Abbot: David and Charles, 1970.

Mowll, Jack. 1980. Personal communications of March 11 and May 21.

Needham, Joseph. 1971. *Science and Civilisation in*

China, v. 4, *Physics and Physical Technology*, pt. 3, *Civil Engineering and Nautics*. Cambridge: The University Press.

Neyret, R. P. J. 1970. "Boats of the Philippines." *Neptunia* 97:1–12.

Nishimura, Shenji. 1925. *Ancient Rafts of Japan*. Tokyo: Waseda University Press.

Nooteboom, C. 1932. *De Boomstamkano in Indonesie*. Leiden: E. J. Brill.

———. 1952. *Trois Problemes d'Ethnologie Maritime*. Rotterdam: Maritiem Museum Prins Hendrik.

Norwood, Joseph. 1976. "Boat Speed Varies with Cosine Squared of Angle of Heel." *AYRS Journal* 83A:5–6.

———. 1979. *High Speed Sailing*. New York: Dodd, Mead.

Paris, F. E. 1841–1843. *Essai sur la construction navale des peuples extra-Europeens*. Paris: Arthus Bertrand.

———. 1882–1908. *Souvenirs de Marine*. 6 vols. Paris: Gauthier-Villars.

Paris, Pierre. 1955. *Esquisse d'une Ethnographie Navale des Peuples Annamites*. Rotterdam: Maritiem Museum Prins Hendrik.

Pawley, Andrew, and R. Green. 1975. "Dating the Dispersal of the Oceanic Languages." *Oceanic Linguistics* 12:1–67.

Peralta, Jesus T. 1980. "Ancient Mariners of the Philippines." *Archaeology* 33(5):41–48.

Phillips-Birt, Douglas. 1962. *Fore and Aft Sailing Craft*. London: Seeley, Service.

Plinius Secundus C. 1855. *The Natural History of Pliny*, vol. II. Trans. J. Bostock and H. T. Riley. London: H. G. Bohn.

Poujade, J. 1946. *La Route des Indes et ses Navires*. Paris: Payot.

Pritchett, R. T. 1899. *Pen and Pencil Sketches of Shipping and Craft All Round the World*. London: Edward Arnold.

Remote Area Conflict Information Center. 1967*a*. *Blue Book of Coastal Vessels, South Vietnam*. Columbus, Ohio: Battelle Memorial Institute.

———. 1967*b*. *Blue Book of Coastal Vessels, Thailand*. Columbus, Ohio: Battelle Memorial Institute.

Shutler, Richard, Jr., and J. C. Marck. 1975. "On the Dispersal of the Austronesian Horticulturists." *Archaeology and Physical Anthropology in Oceania* 10:81–113.

———, and M. E. Shutler. 1975. *Oceanic Prehistory*. Menlo Park, Calif.: Cummings.

Smyth, H. Warington. 1895. *Notes of a Journey on the Upper Mekong, Siam*. London: J. Murray.

———. 1929. *Mast and Sail in Europe and Asia*. London: Blackwood.

Sopher, David E. 1957–1959. *Geography of Indian Coasts*. Annual Summary Reports, Office of Naval Research, NR 388–041. Sacramento, Calif.: author's manuscript duplicate.

Stover, Harry B. 1978. "Catamaran Stability." *Journal of the Experimental Yacht Society*, No. 6:12–20.

Suder, Dr. Hans. 1930. *Vom Einbaum und Floss zum Schiff*. Veröffentlichungen des Instituts für Meereskunde, Neue Folge B. Historisch-volkswirt-schaftliche Reihe. Heft 7. Berlin: E. S. Mittler und Sohn.

Villiers, Alan. 1957. "The Marvelous Maldive Islands." *National Geographic* 111:829–849.

Wallace, Alfred R. 1869. *The Malay Archipelago*. New York: Harper and Bros.

Webb, Walter Prescott. 1951. "An Honest Preface." *Southwest Review* 36:312–314.

Wernstedt, F. L., and J. Spencer. 1967. *The Philippine Island World*. Berkeley: University of California Press.

Worcester, G. R. G. 1971. *The Junks and Sampans of the Yangtze*. Annapolis, Md.: Naval Institute Press.

Index

African Negroid peoples, 49
African outriggers, 47, 79–80
age-area hypothesis, 20, 46, 48, 73–74
ages: according to Haddon and Hornell, 47, 48; Austro-
    nesian canoes, 92–93; bark boats, 74, 89; common
    spritsail, 85; crane spritsail, 80–83; double canoe, 76,
    89–90; double outrigger canoe, 79, 92; double sprit-
    sail, 80; dugout, 75, 76, 89; Oceanic spritsail, 80–83;
    primitive lugsail, 84; raft, 74, 89; rectangular boom
    lugsail, 84; shunting, 78–79, 90–92; single-outrigger
    canoe, 76–79, 89–90; square boom lugsail, 84; tack-
    ing, 78, 89–90; trapezial boom lugsail, 84
Amateur Yacht Research Society, 36 n
Amboina, 65
Amphlett Islands, 24
angle of attack, float, 65
Angola, 74
Annam, 85, 92. See also Indochina; Vietnam
archaeology, in Austronesia, 51
aspect ratio of sails, 83
asymmetry, hull, 29–30, 87–88
Australia, 23, 49, 51, 52, 74, 76, 79, 89
Australoid peoples, 49–51
Austronesian language phylum, 19–20, 49, 52
Austronesian peoples, 46, 47–48, 49, 52, 76, 84

balance board, 68, 92
balance lugsail. See rectangular boom lugsail
Bali, 30
bark boats, 23, 51, 74, 76, 80, 89
beam-to-depth ratios, 55
betel people, 48
bilateral symmetry, 29. See also symmetry; asymmetry
Bismarcks, 51, 52, 84, 88
boom lugsail, 44–45, 80–84
Borneo, 74
Boro Bodur, 47, 74, 92

Boro Bodur balance lugsail. See rectangular boom lugsail
Bruce numbers, 62–63, 66

canoes: ages of, 21, 46–48, 54, 72, 76–80, 92–93; archaeo-
    logical, 74; cognates of, 19; complexity of, 86–87;
    construction of, 55, 61–62; development of, 51; dis-
    tribution and age of, 76–80; Doran's age hypothesis
    of, 21, 92–93; Haddon and Hornell's age hypothesis
    of, 46–48; materials in, 55, 61–62; origins of, 46–47;
    seaworthiness and age of, 54, 72; sizes of, 55; speeds
    of, 62–68; stability of, 56–61, 62; types of, 45
Canoes of Oceania, 46, 47
canted squaresail. See rectangular boom lugsail
Cape York, 79, 92
capsize rate, 68–69
capsizing forces (wind and rig), 56
cargoes, in Pacific, 55
Carolines, 62, 88
catamaran, 24, 59, 68. See also double canoe
Caucasoid peoples, 49
center of effort, sail, 29, 30
Ceylon, 49. See also Sri Lanka
China, 39, 49, 55, 76, 84, 85
claw sail. See Oceanic spritsail
Collingwood Bay, 92
common spritsail, 39, 84, 85
computer simulation of voyages, 20
controlled voyages of discovery, 20
Cook, Captain James, 41, 83
course made good, 36
crane spritsail, 41–44, 45, 80–83
crew weight, 56, 68
cultural progression, assumption of, 72
culture areas, of Oceania, 49

Dar es Salaam, 47
dating techniques, 73

decks, 55
density of water and air, 68
diffusion, 73
dipping lugsail. *See* rectangular boom lugsail
displacement, 55
distribution: bark boat, 74; boom lugsail, 80–84; canoe complexity, 86–87; common spritsail, 84; crane spritsail, 80–83; double canoe, 76; double-outrigger canoe, 76, 79–80; double spritsail, 80; dugout, 75; end symmetry, 87–88; hull asymmetry, 88; Oceanic spritsail, 80–83; primitive lugsail, 83; quarter rudder, 85–86; raft, 74; rectangular boom lugsail, 83; shunting, 78–79; single-outrigger canoe, 76–79; sponson, 86, 92; square boom lugsail, 83; tacking, 78; trapezial boom lugsail, 83
Dongson culture, 92
double canoe: age of, 76, 80; disappearance of, in Melanesia and Micronesia, 71; disappearance of, in Polynesia, 24, 62; description of, 24–29; distribution of, 45, 48, 76, 89–90; as *tongiaki* in Tonga, 43–44; relict distribution of, 76, 89, 90
double-outrigger canoe: age of, 79–80; description of, 30, 33–35; distribution of, 45, 48, 76, 79–80, 92; stability of, 30
double spritsail, 39, 80
drag, 56, 69
drift voyage hypothesis, 20
dugout, 24, 76, 80, 89

East Africa, 47, 80, 87
Easter Island, 19, 47, 49
ecology, 73
Ecuador, 24
edge dowelling, 61–62
Ellice Islands, 88, 91
Emirau, 88
end symmetry, 29–30, 87–88
Epifano, 62
European spritsail, 85. *See also* common spritsail

Fiji, 52, 55, 62, 88, 91
Finney, Ben R., 24, 36 n
float axes, 65
"flying a float," 60
"flying a hull," 60
Flying Cloud, 62
"flying proas," 62
"fore-and-aft" sail, 39
Formosa, 24, 87
form resistance, 56

founder populations, 49
freeboard, 55

Geelvink Bay, 65, 92
genealogies, 46, 73
genetic drift, 49
Gilberts, 55, 62, 87
glottochronology, 73
Guam, 62
Gulf of Carpentaria, 74

Haddon, A. C.: canoe age hypotheses of, 47; contributions by, 21; outrigger papers by, 47; seaworthiness hypotheses of, 54; work of, with James Hornell, 21, 46–48, 93
hama ("outrigger float" or "port hull"), 90
Hawaii, 24, 41, 55, 62, 65
Hokule'a: Bruce number of, 65; freeboard of, 55; speed of, 62, 65; voyage of, to Tahiti, 24, 93
Hornell, James: canoe age hypotheses of, 47–48; contributions by, 21; outrigger papers by, 47; and sail names, 41, 43; seaworthiness hypotheses of, 54; work of, with A. C. Haddon, 21, 46–48, 93
Horridge, G. Adrian, 47
Howard, Alan, 46
Huahine, Society Islands, 74
hull construction technique, 61–62, 65
hull shapes, 24, 29–30, 55
hundred-foot canoes, 55
hypothetical canoes, 65–66

India, 24, 49, 76, 85, 89
Indian Ocean, 39
Indochina, 49, 83–84. *See also* Annam; Vietnam
Indonesia: canoe speeds in, 62; canoe types of, 30, 45, 76–78; covariation in race and language of, 52; distribution of sail types in, 83, 85; double outrigger distribution in, 47, 48, 92; dugouts in, 76; edge dowel construction in, 61–62; human characteristics of, 49; papers and monographs on, 47, 48; relict double canoes and single outriggers of, 78, 90; scarfs in, 61; seaworthiness of canoes of, 72; shunting in, 87, 88; traders of, 92
Indonesian lugsail. *See* rectangular boom lugsail
Indonesian spritsail. *See* double spritsail
inverted triangular sail. *See* Oceanic spritsail

Java, 30, 65, 80
junks, 92

katea ("main hull"), 90

katig (outrigger float name), 84
"kava people," 46, 48

Lamu, 47
languages, 19–20, 49, 51
Lapita pottery, 51–52, 90
lashing stresses, 67
lateen sail, 41–43
layag sail. *See* rectangular boom lugsail
leeway boards, 24
leha sail. *See* rectangular boom lugsail
length-to-beam ratios, 55–56
Lewis, David, 20, 36 n, 41
lines drawings, 24, 29–30
linguistics, 19–20, 21, 51, 88
log boat. *See* dugout
Louisiades, 80, 92
lugsail, 39, 44–45
lyre tanjong sail. *See* rectangular boom lugsail

Madagascar, 47, 49, 78, 79, 80, 87, 89, 91
Mailu, 24, 91
Makassar, 65
Malaya, 83
Malayo-Polynesian. *See* Austronesian language phylum
Maldives, 80
Mangareva, 23
Manihiki, 43, 44
Manila, 62, 65, 83
Manokwari, 65
Manureva, 63
Mapia Islands, 88
Marianas, 88
Marquesas, 47, 52, 61
Marshall Islands, 88
Mediterranean, 41
Melanesia: canoe types of, 45, 76; characteristics of, 49; pre-Polynesian trading in, 52; race and language of, 52; relict double canoes in, 76, 90; sail types of, 43, 45, 83; seaworthiness of canoes of, 72; shunting in, 78–79, 87
Menado (Sulawesi), 65
Micronesia: canoe speeds in, 62; canoe types of, 29–30, 45; characteristics of, 49; development of canoes in, 21; "flying the float" in, 60; hull asymmetry in, 88; race and language of, 52; righting technique in, 56; seaworthiness of canoes of, 72; shunting in, 87, 88, 91; single-outrigger canoe in, 29–30, 78–79; spritsails of, 43, 83
migration theories, 52

Mikael, 55, 62–65, 66
Minahasa, 62
Mindanao, 74, 83
Moluccas, 55, 92
mon canoe, 48, 92
Mongoloid peoples, 49
Morwood, John, 36 n

Nalehia, 24, 55, 60, 62–65, 66
Nardi, 62–65
nautical vocabulary, 23, 39
navigation, in Pacific, 20–21
New Britain, 88
New Caledonia, 52, 88, 91
New Guinea, 46, 49, 51, 76, 80, 86, 87, 92
New Hebrides, 52, 74, 80, 88
New Ireland, 88
New South Wales, 74
New Zealand, 61, 76
Niah caves, 74
Nissan, 80, 92
Nooteboom, C., 47
Novaliches pottery, 92

oblong mat sail. *See* rectangular boom lugsail
obsidian, 52
Oceania, 49, 52, 55
Oceanic lateen sail, 47. *See also* crane spritsail
Oceanic spritsail: age of, 47, 80–83; description of, 39–41; distribution of, 45, 48, 80–83; relationship of, to crane spritsail, 43
"Old Melanesia," 51, 74
Ondine III, 62–63
orembai boat, 92
origins: of double canoes, 90; of double-outrigger canoes, 92; of Pacific islanders, 19; of shunting, 91; of single-outrigger canoes, 90
orou canoe, 24, 93
outrigger origins, theories of, 47

Pacific culture history, 19–20, 43, 49–52
Palau, 47, 88
Papua, 24, 41
Papuan language phyla, 19, 49
Paris, F. E., 24, 65
Philippines, 65, 66, 83, 84
physical anthropology, 49
polar speed diagram, 63–64
poling, 48
Polynesia: canoe speeds in, 62; canoe types of, 45, 76;

characteristics of, 49; culture-history theories for, 52; disappearance of double canoes from, 24; race, languages, and culture of, 51, 52; seaworthiness of canoes of, 72; shunting in, 87, 91; spritsails of, 43; use of balance board in, 68

preservation, canoe, 74

primitive crane spritsail. *See* crane spritsail

primitive lateen sail. *See* crane spritsail

primitive rectangular lugsail, 83, 84. *See also* rectangular boom lugsail

proa, 29, 59, 61, 68, 69. *See also* single-outrigger canoe

proto-Austronesian language, 19, 84, 90

proto-Mongoloid peoples, 49, 51, 52, 90

proto-Oceanic spritsail. *See* double spritsail

Puluwat Atoll, 30, 62

quadrangular sail, 47. *See also* rectangular boom lugsail

quadrilateral sail. *See* rectangular boom lugsail

quarter rudder, 78, 85–86, 92

Queensland, 46

races, 49

radial inertia, 68

radiocarbon dating, 20, 49, 73

rafts, 23–24, 74, 76, 80, 89

rectangular boom lugsail, 44–45, 83, 84

rectangular lugsail. *See* rectangular boom lugsail

rectangular spritsail. *See* double spritsail

Reef Islands, 41

relicts, 76, 78, 90, 93

righting force, 56

righting technique, 56

Rossell Island, 88

safety factor, 60–61

Sahul Shelf, 51

sail balance, 29, 69–71

sail nomenclature, 39, 41, 44

sail types, 39–45, 47

sama (outrigger float name), 84

Samoa, 51, 88, 89, 91

Santa Cruz Islands, 52, 88

scarfs, 61, 62

Schouten, Willem Cornelis, 83

sea levels, in Pleistocene, 51

seaworthiness: ambiguity of, 34; Bruce numbers and, 62–63, 66; and crew weight, 68; and decks and freeboard, 55; differences in, 61–71; and displacement, 55; and hull construction, 61–62; and hull form, 55; hypotheses about, 54, 72; and materials, 55; rank order of, 54, 71–72; and rate of capsize, 68–69; and righting ability, 56; and sail balance, 69–71; similarities in, 54–61; and size, 55; and speed, 56, 62–68; and stability, 56–61, 67–68; summary of, 71–72

seed agriculture, 49, 52

sheet steering, 79

shunting: age of, 78, 80; definition of, 36; distribution of, 78–79, 90–91; movement eastward of, 44, 91

single-outrigger canoe: absence of, in mainland Southeast Asia, 78; age of, 78, 80; balance board on, 68; description of, 29–30; distribution of, 45, 76–79, 89–91; relict distribution of, 78, 80, 89

skin friction, 56

Society Islands, 74

Solomons, 48, 55, 88, 92

sompot sail. *See* rectangular boom lugsail

speed differences: design for, 67; estimated, 62–63; historic sources on, 62; hypothetical, 65–68; measured, 63–65

sponsons, 48, 86

spritsail, 39, 78

square boom lugsail, 45, 83, 84

square sail, 39, 48

Sri Lanka, 78–79, 80, 86, 87, 91

stability, 56–61

stability curves, 59–61, 71

standing lugsail. *See* rectangular boom lugsail

stern rudders, 85–86

Stover, Harry B., 59

stratification, 73

Sulawesi, 21, 30, 62, 65, 87, 91

Sulu, 24, 30, 55, 62, 65

Sumatra, 83

Sunda Shelf, 51

symmetry, hull, 29–30, 87–88

tacking, 36, 78, 80, 90

Tahiti, 24, 30, 55, 56, 65

Taiwan. *See* Formosa

Talasea Peninsula (New Britain), 52

Tasman, Abel, 83

Tasmania, 23, 51, 74, 89

toe-out of floats. *See* float axes

Tokelaus, 91

Tonga, 23, 43, 44, 51, 83, 88, 89, 90, 91

topsides, Hawaiian, 24

Torres Strait, 92

trapezial boom lugsail, 45, 83, 84

trimaran, 30, 59, 68, 69. *See also* double-outrigger canoe

Trobriand Islands, 92
Tuamotus, 24, 43, 44, 55, 74, 83, 87, 88, 90
typological cline, 83

Vietnam, 21, 24, 83, 86, 92. *See also* Annam;
    Indochina
vinta, 30, 62–65
voyaging conditions, 62

Waigeo, 65
wangka, meaning of, 19
wash strake, 24, 55
Water Transport, 48
wave theory of migration, 46–48, 51
western craft, 55

Yap, 23, 92